Theorizing Global Order

Normative Orders

Publications of the Cluster of Excellence "The Formation of Normative Orders" at Goethe University, Frankfurt am Main

Edited by Rainer Forst and Klaus Günther

Volume 22

Gunther Hellmann is Professor of Political Science at Goethe University, Frankfurt am Main.

Gunther Hellmann (ed.)

Theorizing Global Order

The International, Culture and Governance

Campus Verlag
Frankfurt/New York

This publication is part of the DFG-funded Cluster of Excellence "The Formation of Normative Orders" at Goethe University Frankfurt am Main.

ISBN 978-3-593-50882-5 Print
ISBN 978-3-593-43855-9 E-Book (PDF)

All rights reserved. No part of this book may be reproduced or transmitted in any form or by any means, electronic or mechanical, including photocopying, recording, or by any information storage and retrieval system, without permission in writing from the publishers.
Despite careful control of the content Campus Verlag GmbH cannot be held liable for the content of external links. The content of the linked pages is the sole responsibility of their operators.
Copyright © 2018 Campus Verlag GmbH, Frankfurt-on-Main
Cover design: Campus Verlag GmbH, Frankfurt-on-Main
Printing office and bookbinder: Beltz Bad Langensalza
Printed on acid free paper.
Printed in the United States of America

For further information:
www.campus.de
www.press.uchicago.edu

Contents

Theorizing Global Order: A Brief Introduction 7
Gunther Hellmann

The Modern International: A Scalar Politics of Divided Subjectivities 13
R.B.J. Walker

Thinking About World Order, Inquiring Into Others' Conceptions
of the International 37
Pinar Bilgin

Seeing Culture in World Politics 66
Christian Reus-Smit

Order in a Borderless World: Nomads Confront Globalization 91
Erik Ringmar

Diplomacy as Global Governance 118
Iver B. Neumann and Ole Jacob Sending

The Sociology of International Relations in India: Competing
Conceptions of Political Order 142
Siddharth Mallavarapu

Notes on Contributors 172

Theorizing Global Order: A Brief Introduction

Gunther Hellmann[1]

Theorizing international relations presupposes a conception of what the subject matter and its bounds are. We have to have some idea of the entity at the center of our theorizing—the 'international' and/or the 'global'; 'relations', 'systems' 'structure(s)' and/or 'order', just to name a few. Of course, *political orders* have been at the center of political theory since antiquity. However, compared to efforts at theorizing 'international relations' or 'international systems', the notion of international and/ or global 'order' has remained surprisingly undertheorized, exceptions notwithstanding.

This volume offers different contemporary perspectives on *theorizing global order*. It is the result of a lecture series organized by the Frankfurt 'Center of Excellence' 'Formation of Normative Orders'.[2] The aim of the lecture series (and the chapters in this volume) was not to offer 'a new theory' (or, for that matter, 'alternative theories') of international or global order. Rather, by shedding novel light at different dimensions of ordering international (and global) politics—both in terms of alternative ordering *perspectives* and alternative ordering *arrangements*—the volume as a whole aims at taking the double meaning of order(ing) as "fact" and "value"[3] seriously.

From a conceptual history point of view the notion of order has always carried the dual meaning of order as (more or less arbitrary) arrangement (Greek *táxis*) and order as natural and nurtured whole (*kósmos*).[4] In modern forms of IR theorizing this dual semantic has lived on in Realist (presumably purely analytical) notions of order 'in' (or 'under') 'anarchy'[5] and more

---

1 I am grateful to Daniel Fehrmann for his support in finalizing this manuscript.
2 On the notion of 'normative orders' see Forst and Günther, Die Herausbildung normativer Ordnungen.
3 Hurrell, *On Global Order*, 2.
4 Anter, *Die Macht der Ordnung*, 22.
5 See Kenneth Waltz's famous notion of "order without an orderer", Waltz, *Theory of International Politics*, 89.

or less explicitly normative forms of theorizing reaching from constitutional[6] or societal notions[7] of international order to all-encompassing notions of a juridically stabilized imperial capitalist order[8] or discursively shaped orders of truth and power in the form of practices and techniques of government extending well beyond the nation state.[9]

One of the underlying assumptions of this volume is that the theorization of 'order' entails an ordering semantic where the dual meanings of order(ing) as 'fact' *and* 'value' (or: of *táxis* and *kósmos*) are inseparably embedded even if analytical or normative dimensions may play a bigger (or lesser) role depending on epistemological preferences. This semantic of order(ing) guides our ways of theorizing order in different forms. First, 'factually' it shapes our ways of *describing* (or: making sense of) ordering arrangements (ie. how things belonging to the realm of the international are to be named and how they hang together). To order thought about the international in terms of 'system' *versus* 'state' *versus* 'the individual' may come naturally to the IR theorist *trained* (in Wittgenstein's sense[10]) to internalize a certain language game about the fundamental arrangements of 'world order'. Yet this type of "'levels' thinking"[11] may be quite problematic from other perspectives.[12] 'Normatively" the semantic of order(ing) also shapes our ways of *prescribing* how the structures, practices and arrangements in the international realm *should* be distinguished and how they should hang together when we conceive of orders in terms of their 'building'.

Second, the semantic of order(ing) also entails a temporal dimension in that it may either emphasize static or ahistorical 'structural' aspects in contrast to dynamic, events-based or historical 'processual' aspects of becoming. Theorizing order as structure tends to emphasize stability and inevitability, theorizing order(ing) as practice focuses on patterns of intentional steering as well as (intentional and unintentional) interactional outcomes. Being aware of these dimensions of theorizing international or global order(ing) is crucial, especially in times when prevailing conceptions of

---

6 Ikenberry, *After Victory*.
7 Bull, *The Anarchical Society*; Buzan, *From International to World Society*.
8 Hardt and Negri, *Empire*, 3–21.
9 Foucault, *Power*, eg. 15, 94–95, 132.
10 Wittgenstein, *Philosophical Investigations*, eg. §§5, 6, 9, 27.
11 Wendt, *Social Theory of International Politics*, 13.
12 Campbell, *Writing Security*, 43–46.

order (or "systemic totality"[13]) are turned upside down. The contributions to this volume provide for a diverse set of systematically reflected ways of theorizing global order.

Overview of the Volume

The first chapter by *R.B.J. Walker* tackles the underlying concepts of order, global and theorization against the background of a notion of 'the modern international'. He argues that debates about connections between the concepts of 'order', 'global' and 'theorization' are shaped by shared but conflicting commitments to modern principles of subjectivity and self-determination. These commitments rest on specific claims about spatiotemporal origins and boundaries. The consequence is a structure of spatiotemporally organized contradictions expressed in aporetic claims to humanity and citizenship, and thus in the contested status of sovereignties expressed in state law and international law. Prevailing literatures usually erase the significance of the spatiotemporal, normative and contradictory character of this historical constitution of modern politics, partly by recasting internal and external moments of subjectivity as distinct spatial, temporal and hierarchical domains, partly by identifying specific practices through which contradictions are negotiated as the primary problem that must be engaged. In contrast to these positions Walker argues that the central source of order and disorder remains the status of claims about modern subjectivity expressed in political practices that must try, and fail, to reconcile claims about liberty, equality and security within a scalar hierarchy.

In Chapter 2 *Pinar Bilgin* asks how we should think about global order in a world characterized by a multiplicity of inequalities and differences. In drawing upon the insights of critical and postcolonial IR she suggests that thinking about global order in a world of multiple differences entails inquiring 'others'' conceptions of the international, ie. those who are 'perched on the bottom rung' of world politics (Enloe). While the field is called 'International Relations' what we recognize as 'IR knowledge' has mostly focused on 'our' perspectives, not 'others'. The study of global

---

[13] Hardt and Negri, *Empire*, 14.

order is no exception. Bilgin suggests that the challenge of thinking about global order in a world characterized by a multiplicity of inequalities and differences challenges on us to re-focus our attention on others' conceptions of the international. She offers 'hierarchy in anarchical society' as a concept that captures the hierarchical as well as anarchical and societal aspects of the international as conceived by 'others'.

Christian Reus-Smit discusses the causal significance of culture in world politics in Chapter 3. In contrast to the impoverished understanding of culture in IR, he puts forward conceptual and analytical propositions that build on key insights from other disciplines, enabling us to understand the impact of cultural difference on international order. Instead of treating culture as some kind of homogenous unit and diversity as the 'space' between these units, Reus-Smit discusses culture's inherent diversity and heterogeneous cultural contexts, assuming four axes of cultural diversity, which can guide the future research on cultural diversity and international order: meaning complexity, diversity of interpretation, identity pluralism and multiple identities. The central thesis is that cultural diversity is the existential background condition of world politics insofar as the institutions of the international order evolve in part to manage this diversity, constituting what he calls a 'diversity regime'. Cultural diversity informs practices of recognition and licenses the construction of particular institutional architectures. Changes in the system follow shifts in diversity regimes. Following the assumptions and argumentation put forward in this chapter, the question regarding the key contemporary transformation—the rise of non-Western great powers and its impact on the future of the modern international order—is whether the diversity regime of the modern order can accommodate these new articulations of cultural difference.

Erik Ringmar reminds us in Chapter 4 that (international) political order based on sedentary societies is a modern phenomenon. As a result of globalization societies have become more prosperous and their relations more peaceful, but people have also come to live more nomadic lives. We become increasingly 'homeless', as it were, and consequently more susceptible to the arguments of politicians who promise to create new homes for us. This is how the 'first era of globalization' in the nineteenth-century was interrupted and replaced by a century of genocides and wars. For the past couple of decades we have been going through a new, 'second' era of globalization, and once again the result is economic development and peace, but also a renewed rhetoric of homelessness. The terrifying prospect is that we will repeat the horrors of the twentieth-century. Ringmar argues that we need to learn to live with rootlessness and that the nomads would be the best teachers in dealing with it because they have no roots; they only have 'paths'. They have homes, of course, but homes that they take with them. We too, Ringmar suggests, must learn to carry everything we need with us.

In Chapter 5 *Iver Neumann* and *Ole Jacob Sending* argue that diplomacy (as 'global order in action') is in the process of undergoing significant changes in that diplomatic practice has gone from being largely representational to becoming increasingly governmental. They specify the contents of what this entails, and the causal pathways through which such a change in diplomatic practice spawns new political orders. Two case studies illustrate their argument. The first one demonstrates how diplomats are now regularly active in brokerage and the facilitation of governance not only between, but also within states. Sovereignty is no longer the basis for diplomatic work, but has been bracketed. The second case study on humanitarian relief and peace and reconciliation work demonstrates how an important part of governmental work, namely dealing with crises, has also been set up in a way that brackets sovereignty. Here they find a general governance logic at work where the key point is not humanitarian relief as such, but governance, ie. to cap crises and resolve political instability to maintain political order. Based on these case studies, they conclude that, while representational practices still dominate diplomacy as an institution, a growing part of diplomatic work is not about representation, but about doing global governance.

Finally, in Chapter 6 *Siddharth Mallavarapu* sheds light on alternative ways of theorizing political order against the background of the colonial (and decolonizing) experience of Indian political and IR thought. Two generations of International Relations (IR) scholarship are distinguished: The work of Sisir Gupta, Angadipuram Appadorai, Jayantanuja Bandyopadhyaya and Urmila Phadnis forms the first generation and that of Kanti Prasad Bajpai, Bhupinder Singh Chimni and (one exception to the disciplinary norm), Ashis Nandy form the second. Their work reveals the contours and texture of thinking surrounding the praxis of political order against Indian experience. Political order in the Indian IR variant assumes several avatars in these renditions. These encompass revisiting specific ontologies and epistemologies generated by decolonization, the strategies of 'new states' given their asymmetric standing in the world vis-à-vis entrenched powers, notions of political 'harmony', unsuccessful attempts at overcoming North-South binaries across issue areas, persisting suspicions of neo-imperial designs of external powers, the ascent and decline of particular species of political order theorization at different episodic moments in national and international political life, perspectives on cosmopolitanism read through spiritual lenses, and a scathing indictment of the unfulfilled claims of European Enlightenment modernity. All of this makes for a compelling brew to renew our commitment to a genuinely global IR that takes cognizance of the variety of eclectic perspectives even within a specific theatre of IR scholarship. Mallavarapu argues that this diversity merits being mapped and then brought into conversation with comparative global slices of first order theorization.

References

Anter, A., *Die Macht der Ordnung. Aspekte einer Grundkategorie des Politischen*, Tübingen 2004.
Bull, H.,*The Anarchical Society: A Study of Order in World Politics*, New York 1977.
Buzan, B., *From International to World Society. English School Theory and the Social Structure of Globalization*, Cambridge 2004.
Campbell, D., *Writing Security. United States Foreign Policy and the Politics of Identity*, Minneapolis 1992.
Forst, R./Günther, K., "Die Herausbildung normativer Ordnungen. Zur Idee eines interdisziplinären Forschungsprogramms", in Forst, R./Günther, K. (eds.), *Die Herausbildung normativer Ordnungen. Interdisziplinäre Perspektiven*, Frankfurt am Main, 11–30.
Foucault, M., *Power*, (Vol. 3, The Essential Works of Michel Foucault, 1954–1984, ed. James D. Faubion. Series Editor Paul Rabinow), New York 2000.
Hardt, M./Negri, A., *Empire*, Cambridge, Mass. 2000.
Hurrell, A., *On Global Order: Power, Values and the Constitution of International Society*, Oxford 2007.
Ikenberry, G. J., *After Victory. Institutions, Strategic Restraint, and the Rebuilding of Order after Major Wars*, Princeton 2001.
Waltz, K. N., *Theory of International Politics*, Reading 1979.
Wendt, A., *Social Theory of International Politics*, Cambridge 1999.
Wittgenstein, L., *Philosophical Investigations*, translated by G. E. M. Anscombe, Oxford 1958.

The Modern International: A Scalar Politics of Divided Subjectivities

R.B.J. *Walker*

International, Global

In the published invitation to this seminar series, Gunther Hellmann offered an elegant account of the broad problem that concerns us. Tellingly, even if unintentionally, but I think rightly, he placed the three terms that make up the title of the series in the reverse sequence, Order, Global, Theorizing, while simultaneously urging a certain priority for the demands of theorizing. My intention is to proceed in precisely this manner.

To state the obvious: each of these three terms expresses many possible meanings. Moreover, the relations between these terms, and especially what we take to be their appropriate sequencing and relative priority, identify many conceptual and political antagonisms of both principle and practice. I thus take the invitation to speak about theorizing global order as an opportunity to sort through some of what is at stake when we make scholarly choices among a broad field of antagonisms that are at once scholarly and political, especially in relation to questions about authority; and I take authority to be one of the important—perhaps most important—of the common denominators expressed in all three terms.

So let me first say something very general about each of these terms before engaging each one in a little more detail. In this way I hope to be able to explain what I think is at stake in making claims about what it means to theorize global order, namely: how to think otherwise about historically and culturally specific forms of subjectivity that are split between claims to citizenship and claims to humanity within a scalar ordering of universalities, particularities and authorities that has enabled us to speak about a politics promising liberty, equality and security. This condensed formulation will obviously require some unpacking, which I propose to do in a way that highlights a number of core propositions:

(i) in order to theorize about global order it is helpful, perhaps necessary, to think about what global order is not, with the most obvious comparative case being what we generally call the international system but which I tend to call the modern international, understood as the twin, parent and child of the modern state. I would nevertheless insist that both terms, state and international, also highlight some of the difficulties of using the term modern in any context.

(ii) similarly, in order to understand the modern international it is also at least helpful to think about what it is not, or at least what it is not supposed to be, which brings us back to the troubling concept of modernity and especially its relationship with the forms of political order that supposedly preceded it.

(iii) conventional Anglo-American theories of international relations provide an insufficient resource for understanding the modern international largely because they rely on a series of sharp distinctions that cut off accounts of an international system from the much broader forms of modern international order of which the international system as traditionally conceived is merely one part.

(iv) what is primarily at stake in thinking about the modern international, as will be quite familiar in many intellectual traditions other than international relations theory, is the status of modern forms of human subjectivity, of a specific understanding of man, especially of the subject that is fundamentally split between claims to political citizenship and claims to some kind of humanity in general. International relations theory affirms both the positives and the negatives of a specific way of reconciling this antagonism, often under thoroughly misleading claims about political realism and political idealism. Such claims, along with related claims about an international anarchy, engage only with some of the consequences of this split, and then in a radically dualistic and reductionist fashion; and this is the form in which a much more complex problem keeps reappearing with some force in contemporary debates about the status of something more global.

(v) Paradoxically, the modern international also affirms an hierarchical structure within which this reconciliation has been affirmed: a scalar order that goes from high to low and from big to small, although, and crucially, this is an articulation of a scalar order that partly resembles and partly refuses the form of order against which the modern international is conventionally counter-posed: empire.

(vi) Thinking about global order very often affirms the basic principles of an international order even while suggesting that we are moving to some other kind of order. This is because of the widespread failure to appreciate what is at stake in (entirely convincing) claims that international order can only enhance greater disorder under conditions that are more and more obviously global. Indeed, the distinction between international and global is a site of considerable analytical and rhetorical confusion.

Before pursuing these and related themes further, however, allow me to forestall some possible misunderstandings by stressing four preliminary points:

(i) Although much of what I will say responds to something we usually call international, I understand very well the force of claims that we need to be thinking in terms of something we should refer to as global. Indeed, the force of such claims has been obvious to me for as long as I can remember thinking about politics; so, more than half a century. The difficulty, of course, lies not in the availability of evidence that might be interpreted as global in some fashion, which is both extensive and heterogeneous, but in the (in)adequacy and deeply over-determining character of the concepts available for the interpretation of and judgements about the significance of this evidence, along with the force of entrenched theoretical traditions that are quite happy to keep working with concepts affirming the necessity of an international order so as to affirm a global order as its necessary even if impossible alternative. Just to take one minor example, Manfred Stegers little book *Globalization: A Very Short Introduction*[1], is neither the first nor will it be the last to invoke the old story about blind men trying to identify an elephant from its disparate parts. For me, the more persuasive that empirical claims about specific trends become, the less persuasive the overall interpretation of the significance of those trends become, and the more incoherent our understanding of what the political implications of what any such interpretation might be. Beware, I would say, of premature conceptualizations that tempt us into too many shortcuts in our attempts to make sense of many confusing dynamics and worrying tendencies.

(ii) While various literatures are quite happy to offer various characterizations of what we might now mean by references to or judgements about the most important dynamics shaping a global order, it is rarely very

---

1 Steger, *Globalization*.

clear to me what questions, or what kinds of question, are being posed when such terms are invoked. The kinds of theorization that interest me, therefore, are those which seek to identify what counts as a provocative question, that is, a question that does not lead to a predictable answer. Easy answers are plentiful and cheap, in this context as in many others, and we do not have to look very far to find their catastrophic consequences in contemporary political life. This is why the theorizations that interest me tend to run up against principles articulated in texts that have achieved canonical status in modern political, social, cultural and economic theory; texts, that is, which provide some insight into the questions that have provoked now conventional accounts of the conceptual and practical options that both enable and disable ways of thinking about what it must mean to engage in politics, or indeed anything else. I tend to wonder about the degree to which the kinds of questions driving the conventional theorizations do or do not continue to be provocative under contemporary conditions. In this context I have long been struck by the degree to which such texts have received startlingly superficial treatment when they appear among theorizations of international and global order: treatments that are themselves interesting for the ways in which they reify a very specific and narrow repertoire of acceptable answers to questions that have been rendered banal as claims about history, and more or less vacuous as attempts to articulate questions responding to very specific conditions that may be relevant now.

(iii) Putting these two points together in very short form, I would say that one must engage very seriously with the *problem* of an international order in order to get a sense of what is at stake, at least politically, in speculating about global order; that is, one must engage with the array of historically and culturally specific questions to which the international order has been understood as a package of acceptable and even necessary answers, at least in retrospect. Nevertheless, one must be very careful about analyses of international order expressed in prevailing forms of international relations theory, including those forms that claim to be either critical or to have something to say about a global order. For me, prevailing theories of international relations are a symptom of a much more serious problem but not a particularly helpful resource for engaging with that problem, though I often appreciate ways in which some scholars manage to say very interesting things on the basis of such compromised resources. I should also say that as contemporary scholarly traditions go, theories of international relations are certainly not alone in this respect. Most of the social and human sciences can be read in large part through the categories and classifications produced by the modern international. Indeed, methodological internationalism is perhaps even more pervasive and over-determining than methodological nationalism.

(iv) Much of what I say may sound disturbingly ahistorical, or worse, as affirming various caricatured forms of history. This is intentional. One of the key themes that needs to be engaged when thinking about what it means to theorize global and perhaps any other order (a term, after all, that tends to encourage structural and spatial rather than historicist and temporal resources) is precisely the kind of history, or histories, we might want to invoke in relation to any of these three terms. Nevertheless, here I will tend to be content to work with various claims about what *must* have happened historically given the terms with which we tend to think about both international and global order now. Our understanding of international order, and global order, is at least as much a product of claims about what must have been the case, of a specific philosophy of history or a history of the present, rather than of any historically credible account of what might have been the case. It is especially a product of claims about an historical break, a great divide between an era before and an era after the creation of an international order. This is a very difficult issue, which I have been trying to engage in other contexts, but here I just want to register that I am aware that everything I will say is in effect a systematic avoidance of it for the more or less structuralist purposes signaled in the title of this lecture series.

Order, Global, Theorization

To begin with, and to come straight to the significance of attempts to make claims about where and when one must begin, the question of order. This is a question that comes in two primary modes, though one might extend the meaning of the term order in many directions. One mode is ontological, some idea of the entity that concerns us, again as Gunther's invitation puts it, especially of the entity that invites the use of the terms global and international: terms that gesture to claims about universality, humanity and the world as such. These are big terms we might say, perhaps as big as they get when speaking about contemporary political life, this side of infinity at least.

It is fairly clear that attempts to identify what such terms refer to attract a contested array of answers. It is also fairly clear that common assumptions that the terms global and international name more or less the same phenomenon obscure some of the deepest rifts among those engaged in trying to understand contemporary politics and the possibilities for political engagement. How universal, and how big, is what we call international? Does what we call global refer to something more universal, higher up some scale of magnitude and inclusion? And what do we mean, in either case, by references to humanity, or the world as such, or the relationship between humanity and world? These are questions that were given influentially systematic formulations by Immanuel Kant in eighteenth-century Europe but might be traced both to much earlier centuries and to other locations. So, to engage with questions about order is not for the feint of heart. Fools rush in where angels fear to tread, we might say; not least, I *would* say, because claims about the presence or absence of angels as the markers of certain distinctions between orders, and between orders and disorders, have played a significant part in the genesis of modern understandings of order, and its constitutive absences.

Another mode is normative or axiological, involving some sense of the acceptability of the order that concerns us. In this case, acceptability is presumably to be understood, at a minimum, both in terms of:

(a) whether the order is to be understood through some analytical, positivist or pragmatic account of whether an order does indeed work in relation to the normalized expectations of that order, perhaps in the way that micro-economic theory is normative (so, in relation to whether it is peaceful rather than bellicose, orderly rather than anarchical, orderly but not at the cost of generating injustices that might threaten disorder, systemically organized rather than systematically dysfunctional).

(b) whether that order is acceptable in some other terms, terms that might arise from within the order in question or from somewhere outside that order, and thus, in the specific case of an international order and its constituent states, terms that involve constitutive antagonisms between internalist and externalist understandings of normative judgement and commitment.

Some of many meanings of the many resonances that come with the term order combine ontological and axiological aspirations, sometimes with some aesthetic resonances thrown in. Consider, for example, in the English formulations, just some of the many concepts-cum-intellectual traditions that have been attached to the term international so as to give a sense of what we are here calling order: structure, system (as in systematic and systemic), form and formation, architecture, constitution, regulative ideal. Already we can intuit the broad outlines of trajectories that take us both from order to global to theorization and from any moment in this sequence to what we call politics. In particular, given the concerns of this lecture series, it is a trajectory that requires that theorization be understood in terms of ontological, axiological and thus political terms before it is considered in more narrowly epistemological terms. This is to take a stance that resists the privileging of epistemological and even methodological conceptions of theorization that have become fashionable in scholarly disciplines seeking to engage with questions about international and global order. It is also to affirm what now appear to be fairly traditional forms of scholarship, despite various attempts to depict these as somehow unconventional and even radical. I would also say that it is also to affirm that what counts as radical, let alone as critical, or even emancipatory, is very much an open question under contemporary conditions.

Put differently, we might say that questions about order lead us not only towards many longstanding controversies about the political, ontological, axiological, epistemological and methodological implications of the term theorization but also, and to jump very quickly to much of what is at stake in distinctions between international and global forms of order, to questions about the relationship between claims about the need to identify a better ontology/axiology so as to achieve a better politics, and thus to questions about the manner in which judgements about what counts as a better ontology/axiology are themselves political. This especially takes us close to controversies associated with some of the canonical thinkers who have been identified as exemplary architects of an international order that can never be global. Thomas Hobbes is especially notable in this respect, not least in relation to his very specific way of framing the (sovereign) conditions under which it was possible to recast the meaning of sovereignty from theological to secular (even if still theological) terms.

Second, the status of claims about a global entity, not least in relation to something we call an international order, or international relations. Here again we can identify two very broad groups of questions:

(i) One about the order that is named as international, a form of human existence structured within a systematic array of inclusions and exclusions among a diversity of more or less distinct states: a form of unity among diversity and diversity *within* unity that attracts a very broad array of characterizations. These characterizations are most easily categorized on a scale that reaches from accusations of a minimal unity, and thus of incoherence, disorder, anarchy, and so on, to celebrations of potentials for a political order of self- determining communities of citizens within an institutionalized expression of a common humanity. That is, this is an order that may not be usefully understood through terms like either anarchy or community/society that push a constitutive antagonism to a polarized extreme. Indeed, given its title, it is perhaps not surprising that, despite many grave weaknesses, Hedley Bull's *The Anarchical Society* remains one of the few useful guides to what it means to speak about an order in international terms.[2]

(ii) A second concerns any order that is plausibly identified as global, not least in relation to:

(a) the general limits within which any order can be said to operate

(b) the specific temporal and spatial limits within which an international order can be said to operate with reference to what we have come to call humanity understood as the legitimate agents of some shared world

(c) the increasingly contestable limits of our capacity to imagine an order within which what we call humanity can be understood as part of a broader world or planet given the extent to which our dominant accounts of humanity have been shaped by cultures predicated on a radical distinction between man and world and various troubled attempts to reconcile claims about human freedom/autonomy with claims about natural and planetary necessities. This is a problem that haunts many contemporary speculations:

- about a multiplication of actors and relations between them
- about the multiplication of and complex character of borders and the changing relationship between discriminations and connects they enact
- about changing relations between stasis and mobility, spatialities and temporalities

---

[2] Bull, *The Anarchical Society*.

- about the simultaneous generalization and specificity of processes that work to appropriate the world and turn it into practices of human consumption, accumulation, distribution and exchange
- about novel forms of governance or governmentality that lead some people to believe that the head of the sovereign has been cut off and others, myself included, to suspect that many sovereigns are sprouting many heads and rapidly reworking their narratives about origins and limits in ways that perplex philosophers, lawyers and historians alike.
- about ways in which politics is being redefined through previously marginalized cultural traditions that might have some capacity to reshape forms of sovereign authorization and delimitation rather than reproduce narratives about substantive plurality within a formal order of universality and plurality.

(d) The limits of our understanding of what it means to engage in politics given these various specifications and their implications for what it means to speak about humanity, or humanities, and the worlds it or they inhabit.

I have tried elsewhere[3] to identify the stakes involved here by drawing attention to the way in which the terms international relations and world politics have been treated as both synonyms and antonyms:

(i) on the one hand the claim that as the largest structural formation within which humanity is organized, even if very loosely, the international order is already by definition global, in a sense that is often taken to be compatible with analytical traditions that prefer to privilege the dynamics of a universalizing capitalism or an all-absorbing modernity under rubrics like a world system.

(ii) on the other hand the claim that because the international order privileges principles of citizenship over principles of humanity because states insist on their own autonomy rather than their obligations to the system that ultimately enables their very existence as states there is no hope that the international can add up to a global except perhaps in the first sense of the broad limits within which the international system can work.

It is not difficult to conclude from a vast array of empirical phenomena that these two complementary ways of thinking about such matters are historically exhausted in many contexts, but it is also much too easy to jump from this conclusion to the further conclusion that we can speak coherently about an order that is global without being international; just as

---

3 Walker, *After the Globe*.

it has been much too easy for some people to think that we have now overcome our dual attachments to the political qualification of citizenship and our perhaps-political but also perhaps extra-political attachments to humanity, species-being, the globe, the planet, the world as such.

Many great theorists have struggled, without obvious success, to show us some way out of this historically specific delimitation of political necessities and possibilities. My basic orientation to what we might mean by 'theorization' is guided by a sense of a responsibility to consider why a lot of quite brilliant thinkers have run up against more or less the same conceptual limits whenever they have tried to think about politics in relation to the world as such and to speak about human possibilities in 'global' terms.

Third, so how to engage in theoretical explorations of all of this? There are often demands that theorization is indeed the term that should come first. This is especially so where political analysis has been driven by a sense that scholarly authority must be driven by epistemological, and methodological procedures. There are often many good reasons for such demands, especially given (i) the primacy given to epistemological traditions in influential claims about modern science, and (ii) the institutional rewards available for research that has strong grounds on which to distinguish between replicable knowledge and something else. On the other hand, there are even more compelling reasons for thinking that epistemology has become a tail that wags the dog, and that decisions about what kind of phenomena are being examined and why they are important have great consequences for decisions about what kinds of epistemologies are appropriate for the examination. Moreover, there is good reason to suspect that claims about what counts as authoritative knowledge share in much the same historical processes that have shaped claims about what is being identified when we talk about an international or a global in political terms. Hobbes' account of the necessary ontological and axiological conditions under which it would be possible to constitute sovereign authority in both political and epistemological matters remains instructive in this respect. On the other hand, perhaps this is an orthodoxy that needs to be challenged, as many have long insisted.

For the time being, however, I will stick with the orthodoxy. We need to be aware of what it is we think we are talking about, and fairly precise about the kinds of questions we are asking about it, before we are in a position to make claims about how we might know it or the kinds of answers we must provide. Perhaps this is enough to acknowledge that not only do the three terms in our title have the potential to explode into very broad fields of definition, classification and dispute but that the distinctions and relations between these terms offer considerable scope for puzzlement and debate that would take us far from the settled routines of established disciplines and scholarly fields. Much of the prevailing literature on theories of international relations is quite vulnerable in this respect, but the unease is clearly felt well beyond that particular aquarium.

International Order

Somehow or another, political life as we know it has become organized largely within the historically rare but seemingly inevitable structure of a system of states, the modern international. Shorter-term historical questions may be raised about the precise connection between state formations and national formations, and the different kinds of order and disorder they required and produced; the hyphenated term 'nation-state' is a vehicle for too many short-cuts in this respect. The differences between the ruminations on political order associated with thinkers trying to make sense of developments in seventeenth-century Europe and those of nineteenth-century thinkers like Clausewitz trying to make sense of the possibilities enabled by the French Revolution and industrialization suggest the need for great caution in any attempt to speak about international order in general. Even greater caution is surely demanded by any reflection on the dynamics of the last century and a half, not least because capitalist forms of economic life and instrumental forms of rationality have not only transformed forms of state and international order but for many analysts have become even more important as the foundational enablers and disablers of human life itself. I would certainly accept that there are already significant limitations to any discussion of international order that does not account for the duality of (inter)statist and (inter)capitalist relations, though not, I think, in ways that undermine my basic point here; but in relation to claims about a global order these limitations strike me as working at a much greater order of magnitude. In a rather longer historical narrative, however, some enduring commonality is more easily identifiable by contrast with the modern international's great Other, the much less rare order of empire.

Despite their heterogeneity, empires are generally associated with hierarchical subordinations of various kinds. The modern international is certainly not innocent of hierarchical subordinations, or of empires, in the plural, but one of the clearest ways to understand what has been at stake in the emergence of the modern international is as an expression of a generalized resistance that characterizes all political practices that attract the label of modern to forms of imperial order. It is in this context, for example, that concepts of both liberty and equality are inevitably attached to concepts of modernity, even if the further specification of liberalism is required to qualify this claim. All 'pre-modern' claims to an above and a below—the standard mediaeval concept of a 'great chain on being' is probably the most familiar exemplar—were effectively captured for a middle ground articulated on a flat and horizontal spatiality. Some things were brought down, some were raised up, all absorbed by some middle point, which then expanded internally and externally on the flat planes of territoriality, property and legal jurisdiction. Invocations of 1648 as the symbolic historical moment of transition get at only a few aspects of what was involved in this respect.

It is certainly odd, and of considerable consequence, that this new flat world of modern man came to be enacted in unison with repeated affirmations of life on a spherical planet. Nevertheless, just like the modern individual and the modern state, the modern international affirms precisely the normative idealization of concepts of man, of humanity in general and as politically qualified versions of that humanity, as, in principle, sites of liberty, even equality, in ways that are at odds with principles of hierarchical imperial order. Consequently, much more is at stake in claims about an international order than the potential for anarchical disorder. Not least is the conception of man, of humanity, that is affirmed against all other accounts of what it means to be human, as well as the corollary account of the relation between the human and the world or worlds he, she or it inhabits. Thomas Hobbes has very little to say about any international anarchy that is so often invoked in his name, but he does have a lot to say about what it must mean to think politically in an age of recognizably modern subjects driven by secular desires, liberties, equalities and necessities in the absence of essential truths, natural justice and higher authorities.

Once modern man is so radically distinguished from everything else, whether read as God, gods, nature or other men, the great plague of modern dualisms must run amok, or so it has seemed in retrospect. Humanisms must work out their ideals of self-creation, or so it has also seemed. The great legitimating force of the modern international in the twentieth century was the principle of self-determination, precisely part of the great refusal of universalizing and imperial orders that has been in play, in some places, for more than half a millennium. The obvious problem with the principle of national self-determination, of course, concerns the relation among self-determining nations, not entirely unlike the basic problem of the relation of supposedly self-determining individuals to their collective expression as community, or society, or nation. Once one arrives at the primordial character of modern man, one needs to know whether one is talking about man in general or man in particular, and what the relationship between these two characters is supposed to be. Indeed, it is difficult to think of many important European political thinkers after about the time of Machiavelli who were not struggling in some way to get a grip on this problem, or to ignore its forceful presence in contemporary patterns of population movement and chauvinistic nationalism.

Like the modern state, the modern international works precisely as a complex orchestration of attempts to get a grip on this problem. The degree to which it does so is the key to which it can claim to express an order with some kind of legitimacy or authority. In principle, it offers what might be viewed as a classically elegant way of orchestrating a spatially differentiated structure of internalities and externalities within which to distribute, bring together and force apart competing claims to humanity in general and politically qualified citizenships in particular; that is, to (eventually) reconcile all claims about the universality and particularity of humanity within a flat but intricately bounded space in a manner that provides secure opportunities for liberties and equalities, opportunities that are not supposed to be available within any singular imperium. Thus we have one international system and many states, one humanity and many sites of citizenship, one humanity and many citizens. Within any given site of citizenship it should be possible for any particular citizen to develop into a properly human being, as well as to express that state of being human in the culturally specific way appropriate to a specific site of citizenship. Expressed as a formally abstract and universal array of a (vaguely) sovereign system of (rather less vaguely) sovereign states, it enables the articulation of more substantive claims about society and nation to fill in the sub-dividable spaces of a flattened world. As with the modern piano, the modern international still sings the scales but on an artfully flattened keyboard.[4]

In this way, both the upside and the downside of the modern international become clear enough. Positively, we can see precisely the ambition for principles affirming the self-determination of modern 'man'. Kant may be understood as the figure most engaged in a heroic struggle to work through the logic of how this ambition might be achieved, through a teleological mobilization of history understood as a force of nature, but also as the one most aware that the upsides are indistinguishable from the downsides, and specifically from the necessity of war. Liberalisms have rarely been able to come to terms with the contradictions that are reproduced and legitimized in this respect. While the opening of a rift between Man and Nature/God involved the critique of hierarchical forms of authority, the articulation of modern forms of subjectivity involved the formulation of new forms of hierarchy. This is an especially complex and rather neglected matter, but some aspects can be noted briefly.

Thus, whereas classical and mediaeval accounts of hierarchy (justice as knowing one's being and social status in the Great Chain of Being, for example) tended to be understood in terms of both quantity and quality (qualities increasing upon going up and quantities decreasing), modern versions increasingly privileged quantity, a single mathematical scale between large and small, macro to micro, a scale heading towards infinity on both ends. This is the scale with which Kant's careful negotiation of a politics of finitude seems to work. But whereas empires and mediaeval conceptions of hierarchy express a great many gradations, a multiplicity of orders within the order, Kant has many fewer. And where multiplicity encourages a view that the difference between one level and another is relatively minor, with Kant the difference is much, much greater, more obviously a site of potential conflict, of wars between states rather than struggles over status. Kant's reading of the problem of international order remains striking. Taking the problem of human freedom as a given, he can read the modern subject as individual, as republican citizen and as international/cosmopolitan, with the possibility of being or becoming human distributed uneasily among these three possibilities. But there is no

---

4 I appeal to this metaphor a little more extensively in Walker, Despite all Critique.

easy movement along this scale, from small to large, from individual to humanity, just three moments of potential antagonism as individuals struggle for freedom within republics/states and republics/states struggle for freedom within a system of states, even while humanity as such struggles to achieve its freedom at the cost of the ceaseless antagonisms of individuals and republics/states.

It is no wonder that Kant was sometimes tempted to reach for an imperial solution, to call for an overarching order of subsidiarity. But such an order would have been precisely opposed to his primary call for freedom to work from within, for history to enable everyone to use their own understanding without being told what to do by someone above, whether God or father. We tend to call it development, which for all its spatial articulation is precisely what the modern international expresses as its necessary view of History. This is how the modern international can appeal both to a seemingly eternal architectural form and yet express all the temporal dynamism that has left its early diagnosticians long dead in the dust. This is also how it can appeal to spatial understanding of architectural form (sovereignty and to some extent statehood) and a temporal view of substantive transformation (nation and the historical realization of human freedom). Still, if Kant is a figure who struggles to understand both the upsides and downsides of the modern international, a status that marks him as a rare and still useful resource in this respect, he is probably not the figure one needs to work through the puzzles of something that is somehow more global.

Four crucial matters are missing from what I have said here so far about international order. This is because I have tried to insist that the modern international be understood first and foremost as a response to specific problems and the affirmation of some very basic principles arising from the multidimensional refusal of more or less imperial modes of political order. Empires have not disappeared, of course, but they operate in the informal shadows of a formalized international order. The four matters I have in mind were arguably all established as a consequence the basic regulative ideal of modern man as both human and politically qualified citizen was in play. One is the principle of sovereignty, both of the state and of the international system, which is best understood less as Weber's theory of the state and many legal traditions would insist as a matter of centralized authority, but rather, and as Hobbes would have it, as precisely a claim predicated on a story about the origins and limits of authority of modern man framed in a very specific spatiotemporality. Second is the centrality of very sharp boundaries, expressed both as geographical borders and legal limits, within which distinctions between distributed spaces of citizenship must be contained. Third is the profoundly contradictory character of the entire structuration, as Kant insisted. Most tellingly, the modern international does not normally permit any binary choice between state law and international law, between, say Carl Schmitt and Hans Kelsen, but always a negotiation between both, at least until exceptions are made one way or the other. And finally, I have relied entirely on the standard European narrative of what the modern international is supposed to be; in empirical terms, of course, it does not make much sense to speak of the existence of a modern international that has any clear claim to include most of humanity until the mid-twentieth century, if even then.

Claims about emerging forms of global order rightly have much to say about all four of these themes, but I would say that most intractable problems will arise once it is recognized that a shift from international to global implies a renegotiation of our understanding of the proper relation between humanity in general and politically qualified citizens in particular. In this respect, all too many concepts of global order seem to envisage a return to forms of hierarchical subordination that might remind us of ancient imperial forms, or the emergence of an indeterminate field of forces that we might recognize as social or economic or technological but scarcely as political in any sense expressed in ambitions for a modern international.

Thinking Like an International

So what sort of question do we need to ask to get a grip on what it means to speak about an international order? Many possibilities come to mind. We might ask about where, or in relation to which time, from which spatiotemporality, does one start to ask questions about order? Or about ontology? Or axiology? Or epistemology? Or politics? One could argue for years about such questions, which doubtless explains the deep reluctance to ask them, justifies acquiescence in some very dubious claims about founding moments and reasonable assumptions and gives some sense of what has been at stake in the authorization of some founding moments, histories and assumptions rather than others.

Slightly less grandiosely, we might ask instead about what really matters, what are the basic 'realities' that drive whatever it is we are trying to explain. Again we might expect many responses, not least in relation to what we have come to understand as matter, materiality, power understood in terms of physical force: the well-known spectrum of claims about political necessity, and thus the possibilities and limits of freedom, liberty and self determination, and, consequently, the constitution of authority. The range of possible responses is no less daunting. Some are formulated in highly generalized terms: power, struggles for resources, control over territory, the consequences of human nature. Most are formulated in relation to a more particular understanding of the character of modern states in a modern system of states, sometimes more in relation to states, in traditions that appeal to figures like Hobbes, Weber and Morgenthau, sometimes in relation to the structural effects of a system, of distributions within a pluralistic array of forces, or a geopolitics and strategic calculations about access or advantage, and sometimes even with due attention to both. Some are formulated with attention to questions about whether the state and system of states are to be understood in relation to the ultimate authority of 'politics' or of 'economics', of the sovereignties of state/international expressed in law or the sovereignties of expressed in wealth and wealth. Hence the many varieties of international political economy, with the spectrum again running from the statist (mercantilism, Weber, Morgenthau, Gilpin) to largely Marxist and neo-Marxist accounts of the determinations of capitalism, with various attempts to understand the relation between two determining logics in much the same spirit as 'Keynes', 'social democracy' and various forms of 'modernization from above' came to symbolize the need for mediation between political and economic processes at some moments in the mid-twentieth century.

While there are many ways of describing and classifying the broad array of theories of international relations, international political economy and even international political sociology that explore this terrain, it is possible to identify persistent sites of theoretical interest. I take the four most important to be the following:

(i) the relation between part and whole, plurality and universality, state sovereignty and system sovereignty, humanity in general and citizens in particular.

(ii) the relations between parts and parts, states and states, sovereign states and sovereign states, citizens and citizens with or without pretension to some shared humanity.

(iii) the relation between equalities and inequalities among the parts, hegemonies and great powers in an order predicated on the freedom, autonomy, self-determination or sovereignty of any specific part.

(iv) the relation between the logic/structure of a spatialized states system and the structural dynamics of some (capitalist) kind of economy; and thus the relative priority assigned to politics and economy as names for competing forms of ultimate value under 'secular' conditions; and thus the interpretation of what we mean by 'society', not least in relation to the citizen and the human. This demarcates the broad spectrum within which most scholars would want to tell us about what it means to speak about an international order. The second and third of these tend to attract most of the attention within the institutionalized study of international relations understood as a normalized discipline. The fourth is more evident outside the more specifically American versions of this discipline and in relation to attempts to characterize contemporary developments as much more than a matter of international relations; so, international political economy, international political sociology, political geography, world history and so on. The first is what keeps political theorists like myself interested in that it speaks to the most basic questions about what and especially who we are talking about when we speak about modern politics of any kind. It is from this site especially that I am trying to work my way through the question of what it means to theorize an international, and thus global order.

But to get some sense of what is at stake in this respect, I have been suggesting, it is helpful to pursue yet another form of questioning, less about the necessities driving the emergence of an international order than about what international order is not. As anthropologists, historians and many others might want to insist, the modern international, like the modern state, is not many things—an array of families or tribes for example. The primary negation, especially in principle, is expressed by the category of empire, understood both as a contrary array of structural principles and as the form against which the formulaic accounts of the origins of the modern international are typically framed. In the specific historical case of the European origins of the modern international, which especially speaks to prevailing accounts of principle, the concept of empire is also linked to forms of empire linked to claims to authority rooted ambivalently in nature (natural law) and theology. Insofar as we are talking about some origins of the modern international, we might say that whatever else the modern international might be, it is not an empire. Indeed, it can be understood first and foremost as a profound refusal of empire understood as a singular even if heterogeneous hierarchy of authority; as not natural (and especially not subject to any universalizing claims to a natural law); and not theocratic (and thus in need of secular substitutes for claims to sovereign authority rooted in transcendental necessities).

These are the three negations that are captured by the formulaic caricatures of history. This contrast is not quite so easy to make in historical terms. Thus:

(a) different understandings of when an international system appeared (any time between the world of Italian city-states and an affirmation of principles of national self-determination in the early twentieth century or even the end of formal colonialism in the 1960s, with the mid-seventeenth century treaties of Westphalia and the post-Napoleonic Congress of Vienna marking the conventional middle ground of an indeterminate spatiotemporality).

(b) different understandings of politics, and especially government, than is given in narratives that privilege the sovereign state as the key invention of modern politics. So while the distinction is historically obscure, in principle it is clear cut. Whatever the (considerable) difficulty of making sense of an international order in historical terms, we know that there must have been an historical rift between empire and a modern (inter)statist order, a rift that echoed in the distinction (equally dubious in historical terms) between modern and pre/non-modern. This is very largely why Machiavelli and Hobbes are the exemplary figures of disciplinary origin. This is also why it has been possible to push the official history of an international order back quite a few centuries before clearly systemic structures can be identified. And it is why, beyond the little world of European experience, it has been possible to insist that the modern international is just the right remedy for all problems that can be encompassed within the broad embrace of 'empire'.

This is absolutely not to say that the modern international is without its empires, or claims to natural or theological authority. On the contrary. But: (i) these claims are permitted internally:

- Empires are permitted in the plural within the order, but not in the singular as the ordering principle of that order; hierarchies and inequalities yes, but a singular hierarchy, a formalized inequality in the sense of a Great Chain of Being, no.
- Nature is brought inside, formalized in the codes of modern science, epistemology and a culture of representation.
- Theology is brought inside, formalized as both Protestant individualism and secular conceptions of conscience and civil society.
- The boundaries of the modern world, of the modern international, are always doubled between an externality as it is known to the modern subject and an externality beyond the inner world of the modern subject and the objects or phenomena it thinks it can know. Many philosophers and scientists may think they have been able to take this basically Kantian form of skepticism to pieces, but insofar as we still live in something like a modern international order this fundamental consequence of a great rift between 'man' and 'world' is difficult to avoid.

(ii) difficulties with the experience of internalization generate many desires to return to universalist accounts of natural and theological law as well as to empire, though understood in rather different terms, usually invoking the world as such, humanity as such, or, in the contemporary coding, something global.

That is to say, we are dealing here with a very familiar problem. The modern international is predicated on a set of claims about the modern subject. The modern subject is what there is. The modern subject is what there ought to be. The modern subject is both capable of knowing what there is and what should be, and on this basis is capable of realizing a condition of autonomy and self-determination within the order that it constitutes. The modern subject is nonetheless a problematic being, in many respects, but two in particular. It depends, first and foremost, on the initial constitutive rift between 'man' and 'world' conventionally attributed to some 'early modern' moment, often a moment of renaissance, when man came to think fairly systematically about the possibility that his own creations were at least as interesting as the creations of God or Nature. This is more or less the moment both celebrated and castigated through the name of Machiavelli, and then increasingly celebrated as both the possibility condition and ambition of modern reason, at least until the promises of human reason began to run into great difficulties towards the end of the nineteenth century.

This is, in a nutshell, the core theoretical problem posed by claims about a global order. In whatever form that concept is articulated, it will eventually get pushed back towards questions about the relation between that particular conception of 'man' and the 'world' from which he celebrates liberations as the condition of a properly human freedom. This is basically what is happening, we might say, in relation to the three great sites of potential transformation that drive analysts to aspire to something more global: the ecological or anthropic moment concerned with the consequences of counter-posing Man to Nature; the movements of peoples that disrupt the international ordering of Man and citizens within spatiotemporal containments of state and nation; and the unraveling of accommodations between state/international sovereignty and the sovereignty of capital that threatens to switch the primary political antagonism from a logic of friends and enemies to a logic of winners and losers articulated in some other spatiotemporal frame entirely.

This rift was expressed almost immediately in a series of polarizing divisions within this modern subject, especially in relation to questions about whether this new humanism involved participation in a common humanity or just in a particular political community; or perhaps both. Everyone hopes for both, of course, but this is not so easy. Again, in a nutshell, this is the problem driving accounts of a modern statist and international order: human beings are politically qualified to the extent that they are citizens of qualified states; as such they may aspire to also become properly human; as such also, they may presume that their own state together with other states may add up to an interstate order that is in some sense an expression of humanity as such; but it never quite works this way, either within states or among states, because the initial premise affirms the priority of citizen over humanity, citizenship as the necessary but never guaranteed condition under which one might achieve a common humanity. Thus the claim to humanity, to an international law, is very thin, even if it is the possibility condition for citizenship, while the claim to citizenship is very strong, especially because it carries the promise of an eventual reconciliation with humanity: the promise that is always deferred so that the promise of pluralistic freedoms is never trumped by claims to a humanity that would be all too close to universal empire.

I think that it is necessary to start from here in order to engage with claims about international order and about the possibilities of global order. But this is only a beginning. I need to make one a final sequence of moves very quickly.

Whose Globe? Whose Order?

As you may have noticed, I have gradually shifted towards a way of thinking that is encountered more often when speaking about modernity than about either international or global order. This is intentional. Part of my point is to insist that international order is not just a matter of relations between states, and that to speak about any global order is to run up against the limits of our capacity to speak about politics in modern terms, even if we admit that the term modern can be made to encompass a very broad array of possibilities.

Nevertheless, the way I have laid out the problem so far is not entirely inconsistent with some fairly traditional ways of thinking about international relations. Some might want to say that all I have done is lay out a gloss on what it means to say that the modern international works in relation to principles of sovereignty. I would accept this, up to a point; two points in fact: the point where I would want to say that sovereignty involves a lot more than the sovereignty of the modern state, and the further point that even the sovereignty of the modern state involves a lot more than Max Weber's definition of the state as a monopoly over the legitimate use of violence in a specific territory. In both cases, what tends to go missing is the broader context that enables the appearance of a centralized authority and a singular autonomous site of sovereignty. Weber's definition is driven largely by nationalist imperatives. Claims about the sovereign state tend to be shaped by concerns about internal forms of authority, often following Hobbes' lead. Though both of these figures make gestures to external phenomena, neither pays much attention to what we would call an international order. Some of the discipline of international relations has followed their lead quite directly in this respect. Other parts have taken the radical alternative of examining the structure of the international system and ignoring domestic considerations. There are exceptions, of course, but the regulative ideal for the discipline has been given by an analytical division between various levels of analysis, with the level of 'man' completing the trinity of state (following Hobbes and Weber) and system (perhaps the dominant disciplinary concern, with many competing accounts of a more or less disorderly form of order).

Many things can be said about this analytical scheme, in my view mainly in negative terms. For my present purposes it works primarily to erase almost all sense of the profoundly contradictory character of international order. Where modern politics works on the basis of two primary antagonisms over claims to sovereign—between a sovereign people (a popular sovereignty, in a now almost forgotten phrase) and a sovereign state, and between a sovereign state and a sovereign system of states (between state law and international law, in the terms that will remind us of the continuing legacies of Carl Schmitt and Hans Kelsen), the prevailing analytical categories simply separate the antagonistic claims at the points of their convergence.

This gives us the possibility of some grip on contemporary debates about theorization.

One can simply accept the radical surgery that Kenneth Waltz and others have performed on the world of modern politics. One can accept a radical division between internality and externality, between a properly political theory and an international political theory, perhaps even envisage a bit of missionary work bringing a bit more community to the international badlands. One can accept the evacuation of much, sometimes even most of the phenomena normally gathered within concepts like economy, society, culture and colonization as somehow subsidiary to something more important. One can even try to multiply the levels, muddy the distinctions, add some non-state actors and novel forms of governance. It is a position that brings many advantages, some in the form of a clear operating table on which to perfect regularized methods and techniques, some in the form of a settled ground on which to articulate normative ambitions. Or one can think rather more carefully about the contemporary fate of the contradictions, antagonisms and aporias through which the modern international has been constructed not as a series of levels but as an uneasy accommodation between competing claims to sovereignty, constitutive distinctions between man in general and politically qualified citizens in particular, as well as between people who are prepared to buy into and live with this distinction and those who are not.

I am not especially antagonistic to much that has been done on the basis of the radical surgery—it can work as both as a useful form of methodological instrumentalism, but also as a systematic myopia and political closure—but I am clearly more interested in this second potentiality. I also think that this option is much more urgent. It is the option that requires a lot of attention to all those sites in which radical surgery has been performed, to the boundaries, limits and borders where contradictions may or may not be negotiable. It is the option that requires some very serious attention to those shadowy moves through which the modern international has been constructed within a world bounded by distinctions between the political and the theological and between the political and the natural. It is the option that works as an expression of a specific account of modern man.

This man has been laid out on a spatial terrain that replaced one version of a scalar hierarchy. It nevertheless still works as a scalar hierarchy, from lower to higher, but within a characteristic set of spatiotemporal limits, within a politics of finitude as Kant might still say. Many people would like to read global order as a scalar hierarchy also, not least to preserve a future for something like modern man, the modern subject. My own guess is that if there is indeed good reason to speak about a global order now, it will require some quite dramatic rethinking of what we mean by humanity, by citizenship, by nature, by the world and by politics. This is a project for theorization now, but it must begin with some humility about our limited ability to imagine a future for the ambivalently human/citizen subject of the modern international if a global order implies some other understanding of the relations between humans and the world in which they live; as it must.

References

Steger, M., *Globalization: A Very Short Introduction*, Oxford 2003.
Bull, H., *The Anarchical Society: A Study of Order in World Politics*, Basingstoke 1977.
Walker, R.B.J., *After the Globe, Before the World*, London and New York 2010.
Walker, R.B.J., "Despite all Critique", in Walker, R.B.J., *Out of Line: Essays on the Politics of Boundaries and the Limits of Modern Politics*, London and New York 2016, Chap. 1

Thinking About World Order, Inquiring Into Others' Conceptions of the International

Pinar Bilgin

How to think about global order in a world characterized by a multiplicity of inequalities and differences?[1] In this paper, I draw upon the insights of critical and postcolonial IR to suggest that thinking about global order in a world of multiple differences entails inquiring others' conceptions of the international. By 'others', I mean those who are 'perched on the bottom rung' of world politics[2]—that is, those who happen not to be located on or near the top of hierarchies in world politics, enjoying unequal influence in shaping various dynamics, including their own portrayal in world politics. While our field is called International Relations, what we recognize as 'IR knowledge' has drawn on particular narratives that do not recognize the roles of 'others' who have been IR's 'constitutive outside'.[3] What I mean by IR's constitutive outside is those who have also shaped world politics, but whose roles do not feature prominently (if at all) in prevalent IR narratives. The study of global order is no exception. This paper suggests that the challenge of thinking about global order in a world characterized by a multiplicity of inequalities and differences calls on us, as students of IR, to re-focus our attention on others' conceptions of the international. I lay out this challenge in section one. In section two, I sketch out my suggested answer. In a nutshell, I offer 'hierarchy in anarchical society' as a concept that captures the hierarchical as well as anarchical and societal

---

1 This paper draws on Bilgin, *The International in Security*. An earlier version of this paper was presented in 'Theorizing Global Order' lecture series at Goethe University, Frankfurt in the spring of 2015. I am indebted to the members of the audience as well as Gunther Hellmann who organized the lecture series for helping me clarify the argument here.
2 Enloe, Margins, Silences and Bottom Rungs.
3 Blaney and Inayatullah, International Relations.

aspects of the international as conceived by 'others' who are IR's constitutive outside.

The Challenge

In a globalizing world, as we encounter, more frequently than ever, those who are not immediately familiar to 'us', we become sorely aware of our limitations in thinking about global order in a world characterized by a multiplicity of inequalities and differences including, but not limited to, gender, class, race, ethnicity and/or religion. Inequality is constitutive of the international, but has not always been central to prevalent narratives on world politics. As R.B.J. Walker noted, IR debates build upon a conception of the international as a realm of sovereign states enjoying certain forms of equality, with often little reflection on the underlying inequalities, forms of inclusion and exclusion.[4] At a moment in time when social theory is seeking to grapple with "multiple complex inequalities" understood as a "complicated combination of inequality and difference"[5], our theorizing about order would benefit from re-focusing on inequalities tied up with differences. For, it is not only civilizational clash scenarios (which prevailed in the early 1990s and again in the aftermath of 9/11 attacks)[6] that overlook the multiplicity of inequalities and differences that characterize contemporary world politics. As Cynthia Weber argued, "both IR and Huntington conclude that sameness reduces instability whereas difference perpetuates instability and that the best way to manage difference is either to assimilate it within the state or expel it from the state"[7]. A particular approach to 'difference' has shaped our theorizing about IR, whereby 'inside' the state is assumed to be characterised by sameness and security, and outside by 'difference' and insecurity.[8] From a critical perspective, then, Samuel P. Huntington's civilizational clash scenario comes across as having adopted mainstream IR's approach to difference and taken it one

---

4 Walker, *International/Inequality*.
5 Walby, *Globalization and Inequalities*, 18.
6 See Huntington, The Clash of Civilizations?.
7 Weber, *International Relations Theory*, 161.
8 Walker, Inside/Outside; Blaney and Inayatullah, International Relations.

step further by "remapping of IR into larger units of similarity and difference—civilizations"[9].

Over the years, students of critical IR problematized such essentialised understandings of difference/s as unchanging pre-givens.[10] Feminist IR in particular has inquired into our multiple and intersecting inequalities and differences.[11] Notwithstanding these important contributions, mainstream theorizing about IR is yet to integrate into its frameworks the study of the conceptions of the 'international' of those who are on the "bottom rung" of world politics[12] with access to less-than-equal influence in shaping various dynamics of world politics (including their own portrayal).

Truly, no procedure is available for entering the minds of others and understanding their insecurities. Early IR scholarship on human cognition challenged the mainstream into recognizing the psychological dimension in shaping the way policy-makers think and decide.[13] Yet, others' conceptions of the international cannot be reduced to individual leaders' psychology, as if human psychology is independent of culture. Whereas political psychology research has, for some years, inquired into the influence of culture on human cognition, IR scholarship on cognition, as Janice Gross Stein highlighted, has mostly focused on individual leaders and "the impact of collective emotions on collective perceptions are not well developed"[14]. While important beginnings have been made in incorporating the study of culture in the study of strategy and security[15], in the absence of systematic inquiry into others' conceptions of the international, it is often essentialised understandings of others' difference/s that have found their way into mainstream theorizing about IR.

It is important to note here that problematizing a particular understanding of difference/s as unchanging and pre-given is not to overlook how a 'stable' identity may offer security to individuals and social

---

9 Weber, *International Relations Theory*, 161.
10 Mcsweeney, *Security, Identity and Interests*; Burke, *Beyond Security, Ethics and Violence*; Jabri and O'gorman, *Women, Culture, and International Relations*; Campbell, *Writing Security*.
11 Lee-Koo, Security as Enslavement, Security as Eemancipation; Sylvester, Tensions in Feminist Security Studies; Tickner, *Gender in International Relations*; Jabri and O'gorman, *Women, Culture, and International Relations*; Agathangelou, *The Global Political Economy of Sex*.
12 Enloe, Margins, Silences and Bottom Rungs.
13 Jervis, Lebow and Stein, *Psychology and Deterrence*.
14 Stein, Threat Perception in International Relations. No page number. Online text. http://dx.doi.org/10.1093/oxfordhb/9780199760107.013.0012.
15 Booth and Trood, *Strategic Cultures in the Asia-Pacific Region*; Weldes, Laffey, Gusterson and Duvall, *Cultures of Insecurity*; Katzenstein, *The Culture of National Security*.

groups. The very notion of 'ontological security' rests on the individuals' need to stabilize their identity through 'routinizing relationships with significant others'. Bringing the notion of ontological security into the study of world politics, Jennifer Mitzen suggested that states may get 'addicted to conflict', thereby seeking stability through leaving conflicts unresolved.[16] My emphasis on the need to move beyond understanding difference/s as unchanging pre-givens does not underestimate individuals' search for a stable identity, even as they incur the cost of sustaining conflict. Rather, I seek to stress the need for understanding the processes of historical constitution of multiple and crosscutting difference/s and the possibility of change in the future.

Students of postcolonial IR, since the early 1990s, have laid bare IR's limitations in accounting for difference/s, maintaining that IR can no longer leave the study of concerns with 'difference' outside its research frameworks[17] and contributed to interrogating IR's limitations and offered contrapuntal readings of world history and politics[18]. However, postcolonial interventions and contributions have remained somewhat marginal to the debates on critical theorizing on IR.[19]

One of those interventions that remained rather marginal to mainstream IR debates is about inequality in world politics. Among others, Tarak Barkawi noted that mainstream IR overlooks hierarchy, as it focuses on the anarchical system of states. This is the case notwithstanding IR's origins in imperial eras, as told by its own foundational stories, he wrote. Characterizing the absence from mainstream IR of elaborations on inequalities as 'constitutive', Barkawi argued that the "absence of empire and hierarchy is constitutive in that inquiry is oriented around sovereignty and anarchy instead"[20]. As such, Barkawi's point echoed Cynthia Enloe's

---

16 Mitzen, Ontological Security in Wworld Politics; also see, Rumelili, *Conflict Resolution and Ontological Security*.
17 Chan, Cultural and Linguistic Reductionisms; Chan, *Towards a Multicultural Roshamon paradigm*; Inayatullah and Blaney, Knowing Encounters; Inayatullah and Blaney, *International Relations and the Problem of Difference*; Pasha, Fractured Worlds; Pasha, Liberalism, Islam, and International Relations.
18 Grovogui, *Sovereigns, Quasi-sovereigns and Africans*; Grovogui, *Beyond Eurocentrism and Anarchy*; Barkawi, *Globalization and War*; Barkawi and Laffey, The Postcolonial Moment in Security Studies; Pasha, Untimely Reflections; Shilliam, What the Haitian Revolution Might Tell us.
19 But see, Jabri, Michel Foucault's Analytics of War; Jabri, *The Postcolonial Subject*; Barkawi and Laffey, The Postcolonial Moment in Security Studies.
20 Barkawi, Empire and Order, 2.

writings where she pointed to gendered inequalities and differences as constitutive of the international. While mainstream theorizing about IR continue to assume the international as a realm composed of states enjoying sovereign equality, wrote Enloe they leave "a great deal of human dignity on the cutting room floor"[21].

Over the years, some other strands of critical IR scholarship also pointed to the ways in which inequalities tied up with gendered, classbased, racial, ethnic, religious and other differences have been constitutive of the international.[22] "The international is already constituted through the legitimation of specific forms of inequality"[23], highlighted R.B.J. Walker. Naeem Inayatullah and David Blaney characterized others' experiences in terms of "international relations from below" that "locates itself both within and beyond an 'international relations from above.'" What Inayatullah and Blaney (2008) mean by "international relations from below" is a "geopolitical space" (as with the global South and/or the Third World) and "an evaluative threshold" that evokes not only externally-imposed "standard of civilization" of the nineteenth century but also the vision and agency of "those below the vital ability of shaping the world according to their own vision"[24].

Let us consider two critical authors who have reflected on inequality as constitutive of the international, focusing on different aspects of inclusion and exclusion. IR scholar Mohammed Ayoob and the literary critic, Edward Said.

Mohammed Ayoob's works focused on material inequalities in the system of states and the implications of such inequality on material power for the production of knowledge about the international.[25] Ayoob suggested that so long as we do not re-think IR from the perspective of those states with less material power, our knowledge about the international is bound to remain skewed. Ayoob challenged inequalities that are constitutive of the international. However he focused on inequalities in terms of material power, thereby leaving other forms of inequality, inclusion and exclusion outside his framework of analysis (even as he labeled his preferred framework as 'subaltern realism').

---

21 Enloe, Margins, Silences and Bottom Rungs, 188.
22 Pasha and Murphy, Knowledge/Power/Inequality; Jabri, *The Postcolonial Subject*.
23 Walker, International/Inequality, 8.
24 Blaney and Inayatullah, International Relations from Below, 1.
25 Ayoob, Subaltern Realism; Ayoob, Inequality and theorizing in international relations.

Edward Said's analysis of the predicament of Palestinian people emphasized what is missing from Ayoob's framework.[26] When Said discussed inequality, he was thinking of the disparity between the 'weak' and the 'strong' in getting their story out so that they would be heard by the world. Here, Said challenged inequalities that are constitutive of the international. His focus was on inequalities in terms of material and other forms of power—what makes it difficult for the 'weak' to be listened to, to be heard. Said's approach to inequalities did not overlook material power disparities, but was conscious that it is not only inequalities in material power, but also other inequalities that remained hidden behind the assumption of equality in the system of states.

Cynthia Enloe remarked how amazing it is to observe "how far [...] authors are willing to go in *under*estimating the amounts and varieties of power it takes to sustain any given set of relationships between states"[27]. Inequalities persist, because some underestimate them, while others are not powerful enough or feel empowered to voice them. While those who happen to be located at or near the top of hierarchies of world politics could perhaps afford to remain oblivious to their effects (declaring themselves to be blind to a myriad of differences, as with colour-blind, gender-blind, class-blind, etc.), those who happen to be perched on or near "bottom rung"[28] are very much aware of how portrayals of their difference/s and their insecurities are shaped by such inequalities.

Hierarchies in world politics are products of not only unequal distribution of material (military and economic) capacity (as with the US as the sole superpower, Russia as a regional great power and China as a rising power). There is also the ability of some to secure access to leadership positions of and shape the agendas of global institutions. Finally, hierarchies in world politics are also products of others' capacity to resist and reshape such portrayals.

Consider, for example, the division of labour between Europe and the United States in deciding the leadership of the World Bank and the IMF, which are viewed by the rest of the world as "two institutions of global scope and, until now, local management"[29]. The same group of states are viewed by those who are on the 'bottom rung' as hanging on to their

---

26 Said, *The Question of Palestine*; Said, *The Politics of Dispossession*.
27 Enloe, Margins, Silences and Bottom Rungs, 186.
28 Ibid., Margins, Silences and Bottom Rungs.
29 Mignolo, The role of BRICS Countries, 43.

historical power to define, enforce, and claim exception to international law and norms such as the norms of non-proliferation[30] and R2P, which was contested most recently during the Libya intervention[31]. There is also the practice of relegating one's contemporaries to the past by way of temporalizing difference and spatialising time (see below).

While it is often the material dimension of hierarchies that are considered in mainstream IR thinking, the non-material dimensions such as those identified above are not inconsequential. Relegating one's contemporaries to the past has significant implications for shaping the way they are understood, and of their own understanding of themselves.[32] As Edward W. Said wrote with reference to the literature that represents the 'Orient',

"[a] book on how to handle a fierce lion might then cause a series of books to be produced on such subjects as the fierceness of lions, the origins of fierceness, and so forth. Similarly, as the focus of the text centres more narrowly on the subject— no longer lions but their fierceness—we might expect that the ways in which it is recommended that a lion's fierceness be handled will actually *increase* its fierceness, force it to be fierce since that it what it is, and that is what in essence we know or can *only* know about it."[33]

Such representations are not inconsequential insofar as they may render some (military) practices toward others possible while marginalizing other (non-military) practices.[34]

That 'we', as students of IR, pay relatively little attention to underlying inequalities and hierarchies, as we think about global order, gives away how others' conceptions of the international has been missing from theorizing about IR. Thinking about global order in a world characterized by a multiplicity of differences demands some way of accessing others' conceptions of the international. The following section sketches out one way of doing this.

---

30 Biswas, *Nuclear Desire*.
31 Grovogui, Looking Beyond Spring for the Season.
32 Fabian, *Time and the Other*.
33 Said, *Orientalism*, 94.
34 Jabri, *The Postcolonial Subject*; Bilgin, *The International in Security*; Bilgin, Temporalizing Security.

Inquiring into others' conceptions of the international

The international, as "a distinct location of politics"[35] is the subject matter of International Relations. Yet, some of its critics consider the academic field of International Relations as "an obstacle to a recognition and exploration of [the international], rather than a guide to it"[36]. This is mainly because mainstream IR has remained oblivious to the particularity of its conception of the international as 'anarchy', and overlooked others' experiences with inequalities and hierarchies, and how these experiences have shaped their conceptions of the international.

Accessing others' conceptions of the international has turned out to be a challenging task for IR scholars. Those who looked at IR studies in other parts of the world were thwarted in their efforts when they found that others' IR scholarship did not always seem to offer 'different' conceptions of the international.[37] Rather, IR scholarship outside North America and Western Europe seems to come across as shaped around 'similar' concepts and categories as the mainstream approaches.

I have suggested elsewhere that, rather than explaining away such apparent 'similarity' as a confirmation of mainstream IR's assumptions of universalism, or a result of misplaced assumptions of 'difference', we could read others' IR scholarship as a response to a world that is already worlded. As such, we would be engaging in 'worlding IR' in its twofold meaning—reflecting on the situatedness of IR scholarship (worlding-as-situatedness) *and* its constitutive effects (worlding-as-constitutive).[38] In offering this argument, I follow R.B.J. Walker who argued that "theories of international relations are more interesting as aspects of world politics that need to be explained than as explanations of contemporary world politics"[39]. More specifically, I suggested that we read IR scholarship outside North America and Western Europe as an aspect of others' insecurities experienced under conditions of inequality and hierarchy.[40]

Here, I take a different tack and seek to tease out others' conceptions of the international from their 'discourses of danger'.[41] More specifically, I

---

35 Jabri, *The Postcolonial Subject*, 2.
36 Seth, *Postcolonial Theory and International Relations*, 29.
37 Tickner and Wæver, *Global Scholarship in International Relations*.
38 Bilgin, *The International in Security*.
39 Walker, *Inside/Outside*, 6.
40 Bilgin, Thinking Past 'Western' IR.
41 Campbell, *Writing Security*.

suggest that we draw upon the insights of postcolonial studies toward understanding the insecurities of those who are caught up in hierarchies that were built and sustained during the age of colonialism and beyond. As such, I take as my starting point, others' 'discourses of danger'. I begin by looking at the case of India's nuclear (weapons) program. This is not only because there is a wealth of postcolonial IR research on this case[42], but also because the issue of proliferation of nuclear weapons is understood to be one of the most significant challenges to global order in its current configuration[43].

India and the 'atomic bomb'

In 1974 India exploded its first "peaceful" nuclear weapon. India's nuclear program had been in the making since 1948 when the Atomic Energy Act was passed. From 1974 (when the bomb was first tested) until May 1998 (when new tests were conducted) India remained a nuclear weaponscapable state that did not conduct additional tests but negotiated at various non-proliferation *fora*.[44] As students of IR we often see little to be puzzled about India's 1974 or 1998 tests. Realist IR explains away India's nuclear dynamics with reference to either 'universal' strategic reasoning; Area Studies views it as a product of 'particular' domestic dynamics. One scholar who has found India's behaviour puzzling is Itty Abraham[45], who maintained that prevalent accounts of the 'Indian atomic bomb' do not suffice, and that understanding the 1948 (when the program began), 1974 (the first test) and 1998 (multiple tests) decisions requires inquiring into the India's leadership's postcolonial anxieties.[46]

---

42 Abraham, *The Making of the Indian Aatomic Bomb*; Abraham, The Ambivalence of Nuclear Histories; Biswas, "Nuclear Apartheid" as Political Position; Krishna, The Social Life of a Bomb; Abraham, *South Asian cultures of the bomb*.
43 Biswas, *Nuclear Desire*.
44 Abraham, *The Making of the Indian Aatomic Bomb*.
45 Ibid., 17.
46 Abraham, *The Making of the Indian Aatomic Bomb*; Ibid., The Ambivalence of Nuclear Histories; Ibid., *South Asian cultures of the bomb*; see also, Biswas, "Nuclear Apartheid" as Political Position. There is also the literature on 'norms' and 'prestige' (Sagan, Why Do States Build Nuclear Weapons), which captures some aspects of the concerns highlighted here while overlooking the relationship between norms and security insofar as they are understood as unrelated concerns. However, as will be argued below, for

In his study on India's nuclear program entitled *The Making of the Indian Atomic Bomb: Science, Secrecy and the Postcolonial State*, Abraham studied statements by India's leaders from the 1940s onwards and pointed to their postcolonial anxieties[47], arguing that the nuclear program was associated with in/security in the minds of India's leadership not only due to (regional and global) 'power politics' concerns (I), or domestic struggles (II), but also due to their postcolonial anxieties (III). Put differently, whereas answer I ('power politics concerns') emphasizes a particular understanding of the international (which is presumed to be 'universal'), answer II ('domestic struggles') privileges the domestic (i.e. the 'particular') as if it is autonomous of the international. Answer III ('postcolonial anxieties'), in turn, focuses on the dynamic relationship between the domestic and the international in shaping one's conceptions and practices of security.

Abraham's research suggested that in the decades that immediately followed independence, India's leaders' insecurities were shaped by their remembrances of colonisation and considerations of the international society as not (yet) accepting of India's independence and/or full sovereignty.[48]

It is significant to note here that what distinguished the nuclear weapons program from the rest of the "technopolitical projects" that also served "legitimation function for the postcolonial state"[49] was its relationship with 'national security' understood in state-centric and military-focused terms. In the post-World War II context of India, two key concepts, 'national security' and 'development' "came to set the conceptual limits to national 'pathways to progress'" understood as becoming 'modern'[50].

As such, the securityness of the atomic bomb for Nehru was not isolated to its use as a military instrument to deter (potential or actual) military threats. It was also not only about proving to the world that India was capable of building its own nuclear weapons program. It was also about portraying India as having 'arrived' at the 'modern' world stage. India's leaders felt confident, Abraham noted, that India could no longer

---

those who are located on the 'bottom rung' of world hierarchies, the relationship between norms, prestige and in/security is difficult to overlook.
47 Abraham, *The Making of the Indian Aatomic Bomb*; Ibid., The Ambivalence of Nuclear Histories.
48 Also see, Muppidi, Postcoloniality and the Production of International Insecurity.
49 Abraham, The Ambivalence of Nuclear Histories, 63.
50 Ibid., *The Making of the Indian Aatomic Bomb*, 13.

be categorized as a 'backward' country that was not fit for self-governance. Having built its own nuclear (weapons) program to entrench its 'national security' just as the other nuclear powers did, India's leadership thought, India had to be viewed as a 'modern' 'nation-state', and treated accordingly.[51]

There is yet another puzzle in India's nuclear behaviour. By not testing the bomb for more than two decades after 1974, thereby maintaining an ambiguity about the so-called 'peaceful' bomb, India cultivated a "nuclear ambivalence"[52] (Abraham, 2006) about its stance vis-à-vis the practices of 'atomic diplomacy'[53] by some other nuclear powers. That it was not practicing 'atomic diplomacy' could be understood as part of India's leaders' efforts to fashion a distinct 'postcolonial' identity for India, suggested Abraham:

"Producing the postcolonial as an instance of, but distinct from, modernity-as-a-Western-thing, is the product of the third world nationalist desire to produce space marked by a specific set of signs, unambiguously signifying the indigenous-authentic, scientific, and up-to-date."[54]

However, from 1974 to 1998, the reasons used when justifying India's nuclear behaviour changed. By 1998, India's leaders no longer seemed interested in portraying India as a postcolonial state that was 'modern' enough to build its own nuclear weapon, and yet postcolonial enough to portray its program as 'peaceful'. Carrying out the 1998 tests was presented as a part of acting like a 'typical' nuclear power practicing 'atomic diplomacy', seeking a place at the same table as the other nuclear weapons states.[55] Abraham maintained that

"framing the decision behind the May 1998 tests was the desire to reduce the multiple meanings of a "peaceful" nuclear program, to force nuclear ambivalence into a more familiar register. [...] Each nuclear explosion sought to reduce further the range of meanings of the Indian nuclear program, bringing it closer into line with received interpretations of what a "typical" nuclear program does."[56]

---

51 Ibid., *The Making of the Indian Aatomic Bomb.*
52 Ibid., The Ambivalence of Nuclear Histories.
53 Alperovitz, *Atomic Diplomacy.*
54 Abraham, Landscape and Postcolonial Science, 165.
55 Biswas, "Nuclear Apartheid" as Political Position.
56 Abraham, The Ambivalence of Nuclear Histories, 54f.

Still, the eventuality that India's leaders sought to erase India's 'nuclear ambivalence' (which had been cultivated since the 1940s but especially 1974), and act begin to like a 'typical' nuclear power, need understanding postcolonially insofar as

"this event mimicked the simultaneous transformation of India's unique state-led economic development model into a more familiar path, the now orthodox global model of neoliberal, private sector–led economic growth."[57]

Shampa Biswas underscored yet another concern of the Indian leadership that was expressed postcolonially.[58] India's leadership framed the international society's objections to India's post-1998 status as a 'typical nuclear power' as "nuclear apartheid", pointing to (what they considered to be) "racial exclusions" at the heart of the nuclear non-proliferation regime. That India's leadership at the time deployed "race as a postcolonial resource" to make a point in the global arena, while masking other "racial exclusions" that allowed re-constructing the Indian nation, argued Biswas[59], pointed to the dual role served by nuclear weapons in the India context.

To recapitulate, India's nuclear (weapons) program could be considered as a component of a security policy of locating oneself in the 'modern' world so as to remove the grounds for less-than-equal treatment by the international society. India's leaders viewed the latter as less-than-accepting of India as an equal member of the international society with access to equal rights.[60] What we learn from Abraham's account of the Indian atomic bomb, then, is how India's leaders viewed this particular military instrument as a tool for producing non-military security in a way that was not anticipated by the inventors of the bomb or appreciated by the students of IR.[61] Given the prevalence, in the immediate post-WWII era, of the discourses of modernity and development, and the claims of some members of the international society of the right to shape world politics on grounds of being 'modern' and 'developed', as opposed to the 'traditional' ways of the new members, becoming a 'modern' 'nation-state' emerged as one way of managing such encounters. The point being that new members'

---

57 Ibid., The Ambivalence of Nuclear Histories, 55; also see, Muppidi, Postcoloniality and the Production of International Insecurity; Krishna, *Postcolonial Insecurities*.
58 Biswas, "Nuclear Apartheid" as Political Position.
59 Ibid., 486.
60 Muppidi, Postcoloniality and the Production of International Insecurity.
61 Bilgin, Temporalizing Security.

conception of the international was one of a not-so-level playing field. Even after joining the international society as members, leaders of the new members were concerned about their treatment as less-than-equal, and sought to remove the ground for such unequal treatment. In India's case, such concerns shaped both domestic policies such as 'nation-state' building[62] and development[63] (Abraham 1998), and relations with the superpowers[64].

Drawing on the example of India's nuclear program, I have suggested that the leaders of India viewed the international society not as benevolent (as presumed by the English School) but ambivalent about their 'difference' (if not 'Janus-faced', see Suzuki, Japan's Socialization), and conceptualized the international in 'hierarchical' terms. In the remainder of this section, I focus on the dynamics of the encounters between the new members and the international society. Where the English School scholars considered this relationship, they understood it in terms of socialization with a hint of 'teleological Westernization'. What is missing from such accounts is how 'others' understood their predicament in view of their experiences with the multiple inequalities and hierarchies of world politics.

Encounters between new members and the international society

Throughout the colonial era (which lasted well into the mid-20th century for some), those who were excluded from the international society had to contend with not only its military forces, but also the culture of imperialism. The latter allowed the former to occur, argued Edward W. Said in *Culture and Imperialism*[65]. The culture of imperialism, argued Said, provided the grounds for some to claim the 'right' to 'better' rule, which crystallized in the practices of 'standard of civilisation'. He wrote:

"Most historians of empire speak of the 'age of empire' as formally beginning around 1878, with the 'scramble for Africa'. A closer look at the cultural actuality reveals a much earlier, more deeply and stubbornly held view about overseas European hegemony. [...] There is first the authority of the European observer— traveller, merchant, scholar, historian, novelist. Then there is the hierarchy of

---

[62] Krishna, *Postcolonial Insecurities*.
[63] Abraham, *The Making of the Indian Aatomic Bomb*.
[64] Muppidi, Postcoloniality and the Production of International Insecurity.
[65] Said, *Culture and Imperialism*.

spaces by which the metropolitan economy are seen as dependent upon an overseas system of territorial control, economic exploitation, and a socio-cultural vision; without these stability and prosperity as home [...] would not be possible."[66]

The discursive economy described by Said was produced through the twin processes of temporalisation of difference and spatialisation of time.

Temporalisation of difference refers to the 'temporal ordering of humanity' in the minds of the colonisers. Barry Hindess traced to classical antiquity the ideas and categories behind the establishment of such "temporal ordering of humanity"[67], underscoring the role played by categories and modes of thought already available to European thinkers of the time, namely ideas received from classical antiquity. Hindess wrote:

"if the peoples of the New World and of the Old came to be located at different points within the one history, an important part of the reason must surely lie in the interpretative resources provided by the classical tradition. In addition to what appeared to be descriptive accounts of tribal peoples provided by Heredotus, Caesar, and Tacitus, the classics provided early European commentators on the Americas with a variety of broad interpretative schema."[68]

This interpretative schema had two main aspects. One aspect was about viewing difference to be "increasing roughly with distance" and another aspect was "inversion, in which case others are seen as being what one is not"[69]. It was through making use of such an interpretative schema that was inherited from classical antiquity, argued Hindess, that 'America' and 'the Americas' were relegated to the past of 'Europe' and 'Europeans'. While 'the Americas' were labelled as the 'New World' in contrast to Europe's 'Old World', in 'European' thinking it was the 'New World' that was considered as belonging to the past. In time, 'non-Europeans' of the 'Old World' also found themselves relegated to the past.[70]

Temporalising difference went hand in hand with a moralising attitude toward the past thereby resulting in what Hindess referred to as the emergence of "derogatory temporalising difference"[71]. Warranting such a moralising attitude toward 'others' was a linkage established between

---

66 Ibid., Secular Interpretation, 36.
67 Hindess, The Past is Another Culture, 328.
68 Ibid., 333.
69 Ibid., 333. See also, Davison, *Border Thinking on the Edges of the West*.
70 Hindess, The Past is Another Culture, 333.
71 Ibid., The Past is Another Culture.

peoples' institutional development on the one hand and moral and intellectual development on the other: "peoples who are some way behind the West in their institutional development will also be behind its inhabitants in their moral and intellectual capacities"[72]. The culture of imperialism in general and the 'standard of civilisation' in particular were produced through this discursive economy.

Not-yet members' reactions to their portrayal as not deserving to rule (by virtue of not being 'civilised') and the interlinked claim made by the international society to 'better' rule took various forms. Some sought to remove the grounds for claiming such superiority by seeking membership through becoming 'similar'. As seen in the case of the Ottoman and Japanese empires, adopting the 'standard of civilisation' was viewed by the leadership as one way of resisting their portrayal by the members of the international society as 'less-than-civilised', and unequal forms of treatment that were warranted by such portrayal. The point being that becoming 'similar' (i.e. 'civilised') emerged as a non-military and non-specific response to the insecurities experienced by the others.[73] Others' efforts to become 'similar' were understood as rooted in their policies of survival, shaped in response to a conception of the international as hierarchical, and the international society as ambivalent (if not 'Janus-faced') toward the new members.

What is significant to note here is that pointing to others' practices of searching for apparent 'similarity' as a non-specific and non-military security response does not overlook the multiple beginnings of modernity in different parts of the world.[74] Nor does it underestimate the agency of the postcolonial.[75] Rather, understanding the search for apparent 'similarity' as a non-specific and non-military security response allows pointing to dynamics of in/security between the existing and new members of the international society. Inquiring into dynamics of in/security as such would allow students of IR to move beyond assumptions of 'teleological Westernization' (as productive of 'sameness') or assumptions of 'autonomous development' (as productive of 'difference') and inquire into the ways in which 'others' are 'differently different'.[76]

---

72 Hindess, Neo-liberal Citizenship, 335.
73 Bilgin, Globalization and In/Security.
74 Bhambra, Multiple Modernities or Global Interconnections.
75 Jabri, Disarming Norms.
76 Bilgin, Security in the Arab World and Turkey.

In offering this argument, I draw upon the notions of non-military and non-specific in/security as developed in critical approaches to security. In the case of Indian nuclear program, as with 'nation-state' building efforts around the world, we observe an attempt by a new member to follow what was viewed as the 'European' example of 'being a state' in the attempt to pass as 'similar', thereby avoiding being labelled as 'less-than-civilised' and/or deserving less-than-equal treatment. The broader point being, new members' adoption of models of 'adequate' statehood should not be understood outside of the context of anti-colonial struggle for some, and struggle for 'full sovereignty' by the others.[77]

That said, what postcolonial studies has to offer to students of IR is not limited to accounting for the dynamics of the encounters between the coloniser and the colonised. While students of postcolonial studies have insisted on broader definitions of postcoloniality, reminding that the 'post' in postconoloniality does not invoke temporality for a particular group of 'colonised' states[78], most of the scholarship has thus far focused on the predicament of the formerly colonised. What is more, drawing on the insights of postcolonial studies when studying those who have not gone through the colonial experience is received sceptically by some. This is surprising, for, postcolonial scholarship offers insight into all new members' encounters with the international society, including those who were not colonised. More specifically, drawing on postcolonial IR scholarship allows students of IR to study the transformation the new members went through as they struggled to meet the 'standard of civilisation' (read: notions of 'modern' and 'adequate' statehood for the post-WWII era) as laid out by the international society.

Others' insecurities as encounters with 'hierarchy in anarchical society'

Here I offer 'hierarchy in anarchical society' as a concept that captures the hierarchical, as well as the anarchical and societal aspects of others' conception of the international. The discussion begins with the English School account of inter-state relations, which emphasizes the societal aspects of anarchy while overlooking the hierarchical. I then contrast the English School's self-understanding of the international society as 'benevolent',

---

77 Ibid., Security in the Arab World and Turkey.
78 Hall, When was 'the Post-Colonial'?; Loomba, *Colonialism/Postcolonialism*.

with the new members' experiences of the international society as 'Janus-faced'.[79]

In English School accounts, the 'international society' refers to institutionalised practices of European states and empires, and the emergence of understandings between the members that rendered 'societal' the relations of states under anarchy. Hedley Bull termed this an 'anarchical society', underscoring the relevance, for understanding the international, of both the 'anarchical' (the absence of a world government) and the 'societal'.[80] From an English School perspective, the institutionalised practices of the members of the international society are considered as responses to a history of unruly relations between multiple actors in 'Europe'. 'Societal' understandings and practices were developed in time to regulate affairs among Christian actors in Europe so as to minimize violence. In time, as Christianity faded (as the source of understandings regulating inter-state behaviour among members of the European international society) it was replaced by 'civilisation'.[81]

In contrast to some other theories of IR that overlook those 'others' who also helped constitute the international, the students of English School of IR have studied the process of the 'expansion' of international society[82], thereby incorporating 'others' into their accounts of world politics[83]. That said, English School scholarship on the 'expansion' of international society does not inquire into the so-called 'socialisation' process as viewed from the perspective of 'others'.[84] Rather, English School accounts are shaped by existing members' self-understandings of the international society as 'benevolent'[85] and assumptions regarding others' interest in being socialized into the international society. In contrast, incorporating the understandings of the new members helps to paint a more complex picture about the expansion of international society and the

---

79 Suzuki, Japan's Socialization.
80 Bull, *The Anarchical Society*; Bull and Watson, *The Expansion of International Society*; Watson, *The Evolution of International Society*; Dunne, *Inventing International Society*; Buzan, *The English School*.
81 Bowden, In the Name of Progress and Peace.
82 Bull and Watson, *The Expansion of International Society*.
83 Jabri, Disarming Norms.
84 But see, Neumann, *Uses of the Other*; Ibid., Entry Into Iinternational Society Reconceptualised.
85 Suzuki, Japan's Socialization.

insecurities that the 'others' experienced in their encounters. A key aspect that shaped those relations was the 'standard of civilisation'.

In English School terms, the 'standard of civilisation' refers to "the assumptions, tacit and explicit, used to distinguish those that belong to a particular society (by definition the 'civilised')"[86]. They were created in regulating relations with not-yet members.[87] In Gerrit Gong's words:

"In the nineteenth century, practices generally accepted by 'civilised' European countries, and therefore by the international system centred in Europe, took an increasingly global and explicitly juridical character as that international system developed. The standard of 'civilisation' that defined nineteenth-century international society provided a purportedly legal way both to demarcate the boundaries of 'civilised' society and to differentiate among 'civilised', 'barbarous', and 'savage' countries internationally."[88]

There was a need for such a formulation, noted Hedley Bull in his preface to Gong's critical analysis of the 'standard of civilisation', for in the European experience, 'non-Europeans' were not always tolerant towards 'European' 'difference' or accepting of them as their equals.[89] As such, Bull suggested that 'European' members of the international society had initially adopted the 'standard of civilisation' to maintain their own citizens' security vis-à-vis the not-yet members. The implication being that if the 'standard of civilisation' was later utilised by some members to justify colonialism, direct and indirect rule, this was not the intended purpose but an unintended consequence. As such, Bull's portrayal of the emergence of the 'standard of civilisation' sustains the English School self-understanding about an international society that was 'benevolent' toward not-yet members as well as new entrants.

The English School's self-understanding of the international society and its relations with not-yet members has since been challenged by critical scholarship that pointed to how it was experienced as 'Janus-faced' by those who were not (yet) members. This is because,

"Many non-European states which were incorporated into European International Society in the course of European imperialism did not only witness the norms of

---

[86] Gong, *The Standard of "Civilization"*, 3.
[87] Bull and Watson, *The Expansion of International Society*; Gong, China's Entry into International Society; Gong, *The standard of "civilization"*.
[88] Gong, Standards of Civilization Today, 78f.
[89] Bull, Foreword to Gong, G. W. (1984). The Standard of "Civilization" in International Society.

'toleration' and 'coexistence'. They also witnessed the European International Society which often aggressively intervened in their land in order to bring them closer to 'civilisation'."[90]

Introducing a 2014 study on non-Western polities' approaches to international order, Suzuki and his co-editors Yongjin Zhang and Joel Quirk suggested that this view of the international society as 'Janus-faced' was not isolated to Japan's leaders, but was shared by many other new members of the international society:

"While it is argued that non-Western polities' acceptance of the sovereign state system constitutes empirical evidence of the internationalisation and global diffusion of European-originated norms in international politics, it is important to acknowledge that many non-European states accepted these 'rules of the game' at gunpoint, and could not exercise much choice over this matter."[91]

Needless to say, underscoring new entrants' experiences with hierarchy is not meant to overlook their agency vis-à-vis the international society, but to highlight the limits of the agency they exercised against the background of their conception of the international as 'hierarchy in anarchical society'.

For example, consider the 'extraterritoriality treaties' that Bull was referring to in tracing the 'benevolent' origin of the 'standard of civilisation'. Notwithstanding their origin in concerns with facilitating trade, by the 19th century, treaties governing extraterritoriality came to be justified through resort to a hierarchical division of world's peoples as measured by the 'standard of civilisation'. In time, extraterritoriality treaties further reinforced the hierarchies reproduced by the 'standard'. Citizens of the members of the international society claimed the right to be governed by a different set of rights and obligations than the peoples of the not-yet member countries they were living in. They justified these claims with reference to not-yet members' failings in terms of the 'standard of civilisation'.[92] Such claims, in turn, allowed for direct and indirect intervention into the affairs of not-yet members. By the late 19th century,

"China, Japan and the Ottoman Empire were recognized as sovereign states but not full members of international society. Their authority over their own people was acknowledged, and generally respected. But Westerners, in those countries,

---

90 Suzuki, Japan's Socialization, 147.
91 Suzuki, Zhang and Quirk, Introduction, 8.
92 As with the 'absence' of citizenship regimes, see Bilgin and Ince, Security and Citizenship.

refusing to submit themselves to 'Asiatic barbarism', were placed under the extraterritorial jurisdiction of their own consuls."[93]

Even after the abolishment of unequal treaties governing extraterritoriality, the 'standard of civilisation' remained in place.[94] Students of postcolonial studies have provided ample analyses of the ways in which the 'standard of civilisation' was utilised by some of the existing members to allow for and justify less-than-equal treatment of not-yet members.[95] Following World War II and the wave of de-colonisation, newly founded states, while recognised as equal members of the international society, soon found that they were "yet to be admitted to its more exclusive inner circles and, as a result, [were] subject to updated versions of the European 'standard of civilisation'"[96].

Such updated versions of the 'standard of civilisation' were sustained by a culture of imperialism. In *Culture and Imperialism* Edward W. Said argued that the culture of imperialism provided the grounds for some to claim the 'right' to 'better' rule, which crystallized in practices shaped by the 'standard of civilisation'.[97] To quote Said:

"Most historians of empire speak of the 'age of empire' as formally beginning around 1878, with the 'scramble for Africa'. A closer look at the cultural actuality reveals a much earlier, more deeply and stubbornly held view about overseas European hegemony…There is first the authority of the European observer—traveller, merchant, scholar, historian, novelist. Then there is the hierarchy of spaces by which the metropolitan economy are seen as dependent upon an overseas system of territorial control, economic exploitation, and a socio-cultural vision; without these stability and prosperity as home […] would not be possible."[98]

The discursive economy described by Said was produced through the twin processes of temporalisation of difference and spatialisation of time (see above).

---

93 Donnelly, Human Rights, 4.
94 Schwarzenberger, The Standard of Civilisation in International Law.
95 Anghie, *Finding the Peripheries*; Anghie, *Imperialism, Sovereignty, and the Making of International Law*; also see, Mamdani, *Citizen and Subject*; Mamdani, Beyond Settler and Native as Political Identities; Grovogui, *Sovereigns, Quasi-sovereigns and Africans*; Grovogui, *Beyond Eurocentrism and Anarchy*.
96 Hindess, Neo-liberal Citizenship, 133.
97 Said, *Culture and Imperialism*.
98 Said, Secular Interpretation, 36.

Before concluding this section, two caveats are in order: First, the argument here is not to downplay the significance of postcolonial studies scholars' interrogation of the 'relevance' of stories about what once happened in Europe to our considerations regarding what should happen elsewhere.[99] That assumptions about the relevance of such stories need deconstructing is a point made forcefully by Sankaran Krishna, and I follow. Nor is it my aim to underplay the need for interrogating the 'accuracy' (for want of a better word) of our stories about what once happened in Europe. As Sandra Halperin reminded, those stories constitute misleading foundations for understanding the study of International Relations.[100] More recently, Barry Buzan and George Lawson argued for the need for adopting a 'composite approach' to studying international history so as to be able to lay better foundations for the study of IR.[101] Questioning the 'relevance' and 'accuracy' of stories about what once happened in 'Europe' (and elsewhere) is an essential component of addressing the limits of IR in thinking about order in a world characterised by a multiplicity of inequalities and differences.

Second, addressing the limitations of IR is not about integrating "'non-European' perspectives"[102] into our narratives. Rather, it is about integrating new members' conceptions of the international (be it 'European' or 'non-European') into our frameworks of analysis. My point about the English School theorizing on the international society lacking insight into others' conceptions of the international is in agreement with Neumann, who identified the limitations of the English School not in terms of Eurocentrism, but in the way English School research agendas were set from the perspective of the existing members to the neglect of new members. He wrote: "A focus on the expansion of international society occludes the experience of being expanded upon—the focus directs attention only to one side of the social relation in question"[103]. Accordingly, Neumann suggested that the expansion of the international society be reconceptualised from "from being a question of expansion to being a relational question of the entrant going from one system to another"[104].

---

99 Krishna, *Postcolonial Insecurities*.
100 Halperin, *In the Mirror of the Third World*; Halperin, International Relations Theory.
101 Buzan and Lawson, *The Global Transformation*.
102 Suzuki, Japan's Socialization, 138.
103 Neumann, Entry into International Society Reconceptualised, 467.
104 Ibid., 483.

That said, so far, there is little agreement as to how to access others' perspectives. For, IR's limitations cannot be addressed merely by 'adding on' others' perspectives as if the ideas and institutions of humankind in X or Y parts of the world have evolved autonomously. They are the 'constitutive outside' of IR. They are 'outside' of prevalent narratives on world politics which overlook the roles they also played in constituting world politics.[105] The new members' conceptions of the international and their practices of diplomacy were shaped by, even as they responded to, their multiple interactions with international society.[106] Capturing others' conceptions of the international requires students of IR to be open to recognising how new members of the international society may have become "differently different"[107] even as they sought to become 'similar'.

Conclusion

I offered 'hierarchy in anarchical society' as a concept that captures the hierarchical as well as the anarchical and societal aspects of others' conception of the international as reflected in their 'discourses of danger'. As we saw in section two, the hierarchical character of the society of states is experienced most acutely by those who are 'perched on the bottom rung' of world politics.[108] In offering this concept, I pay heed to John Hobson and Robert Vitalis' caution that mainstream IR, for all its stress on the anarchical character of the international, rests on a pre-existing hierarchy which goes unacknowledged.[109] While there have been attempts to render visible the 'hierarchy in anarchy'[110] or 'hierarchy under anarchy'[111] in recognition of 'inequalities' between states, their focus has thus far been on material (or military) inequalities and/or institutionalised relationships of

---

105 Bilgin, *The International in Security*.
106 Jabri, Disarming Norms.
107 Bilgin, Security in the Arab World and Turkey.
108 Enloe, Margins, Silences and Bottom Rungs.
109 Hobson, The Twin Self-Delusions of IR; Vitalis, Birth of a Discipline.
110 Donnelly, Sovereign Inequalities and Hierarchy in Anarchy.
111 Wendt and Friedheim, Hierarchy Under Aanarchy.

dependency, to the neglect of inequalities that follow relegating one's contemporaries to the past by temporalising difference and spatialising time.[112]

While Jack Donnelly's[113] analysis does capture the 'standard of civilisation' as an aspect of 'hierarchy in anarchy', his analysis of contemporary world politics does not look at what he regards as 'inequalities without contemporary analogues'. Be that as it may, world politics is shaped by multiple inequalities conditioned by the twin processes of temporalising difference and spatialising time, which shape the way we 'see' the world while rendering less 'visible' their institutionalized effects. A case at hand is how the new and non-nuclear powers understand the way nuclear proliferation is managed by the great powers: as a 'nuclearapartheid'. As Shampa Biswas argued, their understanding of the non-proliferation regime points to the 'undemocratic character of international relations' as regards the governance of nuclear weapons.[114] Such a 'racially institutionalized global hierarchy', as viewed by the new or on-nuclear powers, cannot be captured through analyses that focus on inequalities in material power alone but calls for inquiring into the discursive economy that 'determines' who can and cannot 'have' nuclear weapons. The NPT regime, Biswas wrote, crystallizes the hierarchies at play in ordering world politics in a particular manner:

"the [NPT] treaty and its institutional apparatus reflect and produce a hierarchical global order in which certain states are forever consigned to the 'waiting room of history' branded as pariahs if they choose to pursue the same nuclear weapons that the 'nuclear five', whose possession of nuclear weapons is both recognised and letigimised by the treaty, consider it essential to their security."[115]

The particularity of this way of ordering world politics has consequences for not only those who are seeking to become nuclear powers but all inhabitants of the globe. This is because 'we' inhabit a world ordered by NPT where 'prestige' is tied up with nuclear status, and otherwise these deadly weapons (deadly in their use *and* non-use) are presumed to produce security for 'us' all. This particular way of ordering the world serves to reproduce both existing hierarchies of world politics (by seeking to limit

---

112 Fabian, *Time and the Other*; Hindess, The Past is Another Culture; Jabri, *The Postcolonial Subject*; Bilgin, Temporalizing Security.
113 Donnelly, Sovereign Inequalities and Hierarchy in Anarchy; also see, Donnelly, Human Rights.
114 Biswas, "Nuclear Apartheid" as Political Position; Biswas, *Nuclear Desire*.
115 Ibid., 177.

horizontal proliferation while doing next to nothing about vertical proliferation)[116] and the discursive economy that gives meaning to security under the shadow of nuclear weapons[117].

Hence the concept I offer for thinking about global order: 'hierarchy in anarchical society'—a concept that captures those inequalities and hierarchies that were once codified into the 'standard of civilisation' but persisted even after the end of colonialism, without losing sight of the anarchical and societal aspects of the international that 'we' inhabit.

References

Abraham, I., *The Making of the Indian Atomic Bomb : Science, Secrecy and the Postcolonial State*, New York, NY 1998.
Abraham, I., "Landscape and Postcolonial Science", *Contributions to Indian Sociology*, 34 (2000), 163–187.
Abraham, I., "The Ambivalence of Nuclear Histories", *Osiris*, 6 (2006), 49–65.
Abraham, I. (ed.), *South Asian Cultures of the Bomb: Atomic Publics and the State in India and Pakistan*, 2009.
Agathangelou, A. M., *The Global Political Economy of Sex: Desire, Violence, and Insecurity in Mediterranean Nation States*, New York 2004.
Alperovitz, G., *Atomic Diplomacy: Hiroshima and Potsdam: the Use of the Atomic Bomb and the American Confrontation with Soviet Power*, New York 1965.
Anghie, A., "Finding the Peripheries: Sovereignty and Colonialism in Nineteenth-Century International Law", *Harvard International Law Journal*, 40 (1999), 1–71.
Anghie, A., *Imperialism, Sovereignty, and the Making of International Law*, Cambridge, UK, New York, NY 2005.
Ayoob, M., "Subaltern Realism: International Relations Theory Meets the Third World", in Neuman, S. G. (ed.), *International Relations Theory and the Third World*, London 1998, 31–54.
Ayoob, M., "Inequality and Theorizing in International Relations: the Case for Subaltern Realism", *International Studies Review*, 4 (2002), 27–48.
Barkawi, T., *Globalization and War*, 2005.
Barkawi, T., "Empire and Order in International Relations and Security Studies", *The International Studies Encyclopedia*, 3 (2010), 1360–1379.
Barkawi, T./Laffey, M., "The Postcolonial Moment in Security Studies", *Review of International Studies*, 32 (2006), 329–352.

---

116 Biswas, *Nuclear Desire*.
117 Booth, Nuclearism, Human Rights and Constructions of Security (Part 1); Booth, Nuclearism, Human Rights and Contructions of Security (Part 2).

Bhambra, G. K., "Multiple Modernities or Global Interconnections: Understanding the Global Post the Ccolonial", *Varieties of World-Making: Beyond Globalization*, 2007, 59–73.

Bilgin, P., "Thinking Past 'Western' IR?", *Third World Quarterly*, 29 (2008), 5–23.

Bilgin, P., "Globalization and In/Security: Middle Eastern Encounters with International Society and the Case of Turkey", in S. Stetter. (ed.) *The Middle East and Globalization: Encounters and Horizons*. New York 2012a, 59–75.

Bilgin, P., "Security in the Arab World and Turkey: Differently Different", in Tickner, A./Blaney, D. (eds.), *Thinking International Relations Differently*, London (2012b), 27–47.

Bilgin, P., *The International in Security, Security in the International*, London 2016a.

Bilgin, P., "Temporalizing Security: Securing the Citizen, Insecuring the Immigrant in the Mediterranean", in Agathangelou, A. M./Killian, K. D. (eds.), *Time, Temporality and Violence in International Relations: (De) Fatalizing the Present, Forging Radical Alternatives*, London 2016b, 221–232.

Bilgin, P./Ince, B., "Security and Citizenship in the Global South: In/Securing Citizens in Early Republican Turkey (1923–1946)", *International Relations*, 29 (2015), 500–520.

Biswas, S., ""Nuclear Apartheid" as Political Position: Race as a Postcolonial Resource?", *Alternatives: Global, Local, Political*, 26 (2001), 485–522.

Biswas, S., *Nuclear Desire: Power and the Postcolonial Nuclear Order*, Minneapolis 2014.

Blaney, D. L./Inayatullah, N., "International Relations from Below", in Reus-Smit, C./Snidal, D. (eds.), *The Oxford Handbook of International Relations*, Oxford 2008, 663–674.

Booth, K., "Nuclearism, Human Rights and Constructions of Security (Part 1)", *The International Journal of Human Rights*, 3 (1999a), 1–24.

Booth, K., "Nuclearism, Human Rights and Contructions of Security (Part 2)", *International Journal of Human Rights*, 3 (1999b), 44–61.

Booth, K./Trood, R. B. (eds.), *Strategic Cultures in the Asia-Pacific Region*, New York 1999.

Bowden, B., "In the Name of Progress and Peace: The 'Standard of Civilization' and the Universalizing Project", *Alternatives: Global, Local, Political*, 29 (2004), 43–68.

Bull, H., *The Anarchical Society: A Study of Order in World Politics*, London 1977.

Bull, H. 1984. Foreword to Gong, G. W. (1984). *The Standard of 'Civilization' in International Society*. Oxford, Clarendon Press.

Bull, H./Watson, A. (eds.), *The Expansion of International Society*, Oxford 1984.

Burke, A., *Beyond Security, Ethics and Violence : War Against the Other*, New York 2007.

Buzan, B., "The English School: An Underexploited Resource in IR", *Review of International Studies*, 27 (2001), 471–488.

Buzan, B./Lawson, G., *The Global Transformation: History, Modernity and the Making of International Relations*, Cambridge 2015.

Campbell, D., *Writing Security: United States Foreign Policy and the Politics of Identity*, Manchester 1992.
Chan, S., "Cultural and Linguistic Reductionisms and a New Historical Sociology for International Relations", *Millennium-Journal of International Studies*, 22 (1993), 423–442.
Chan, S., *Towards a Multicultural Roshamon Paradigm in International Relations: Collected Essays*, Tampere 1996.
Chowdhry, G./Nair, S., *Power, Postcolonialism, and International Relations: Reading Race, Gender, and Class*, New York 2002.
Davison, A., *Border Thinking on the Edges of the West: Crossing Over the Hellespont*, 2014.
Donnelly, J., "Human Rights: A New Standard of Civilization?", *International Affairs*, 74 (1998), 1–24.
Donnelly, J., "Sovereign Inequalities and Hierarchy in Anarchy: American Power and International Society", *European Journal of International Relations*, 12 (2006), 139–170.
Dunne, T., *Inventing International Society: A History of the English School*, New York 1998.
Enloe, C., "Margins, Silences and Bottom Rungs: How to Overcome the Underestimation of Power in the Study of International Relations", in Booth, K./Smith, S./Zalewski, M. (eds.), *International Theory: Positivism and Beyond*, Cambridge 1997, 186–202.
Fabian, J., *Time and the Other: how Anthropology Makes its Object*, New York 1983.
Gong, G. W., "China's Entry into International Society", in Bull, H./Watson, A. (eds.), *The Expansion of International Society*, Oxford 1984a, 171–183.
Gong, G. W., *The Standard of 'Civilization' in International Society*, Oxford 1984b.
Gong, G. W., "Standards of Civilization Today", in Mozaffari, M. (ed.), *Globalization and Civilizations*, London 2002, 77–96.
Grovogui, S. N., *Sovereigns, Quasi-sovereigns and Africans: Race and Self-determination in International Law*, Minneapolis 1996.
Grovogui, S. N., "Come to Africa: a Hermeneutics of Race in International Theory", *Alternatives: Global, Local, Political*, 26 (2001), 425–448.
Grovogui, S. N., *Beyond Eurocentrism and Anarchy: Memories of International Order and Institutions*, New York 2006.
Grovogui, S. N., "Looking Beyond Spring for the Season: An African Perspective on the World Order after the Arab Revolt", *Globalizations*, 8 (2011), 567–572.
Hall, S., "When was 'the Post-colonial'? Thinking at the Limit", *The Post-colonial Question: Common Skies, Divided Horizons*, 1996, 242–262.
Halperin, S., *In the Mirror of the Third World: Capitalist Development in Modern Europe*, Ithaca, N.Y. 1997.
Halperin, S., "International Relations Theory and the Hegemony of Western Conceptions of Modernity", in Jones, B. G. (ed.), *Decolonizing International Relations*, Lanham: 2006, 43–63.
Hindess, B. "Neo-liberal Citizenship", *Citizenship Studies*, 6 (2002), 127–143.

Hindess, B., "The Past is Another Culture", *International Political Sociology*, 1 (2007), 325–338.
Hobson, J. M., "The Twin Self-Delusions of IR: Why 'Hierarchy' and Not 'Anarchy' Is the Core Concept of IR", *Millennium – Journal of International Studies*, 42 (2014), 557–575.
Huntington, S. P., "The Clash of Civilizations?", *Foreign Affairs*, 72 (1993), 22–49.
Inayatullah, N./Blaney, D. L., "Knowing Encounters: Beyond Parochialism in International Relations Theory", in Lapid, Y./Kratochwil, F. V. (eds.), *The return of culture and identity in IR theory*, Boulder, Colo. 1996, 65–84.
Inayatullah, N./Blaney, D. L., *International Relations and the Problem of Difference*, London 2004.
Jabri, V., "Michel Foucault's Analytics of War: The Social, the International, and the Racial", *International Political Sociology*, 1 (2007), 67–81.
Jabri, V., *The Postcolonial Subject: Claiming Politics/Governing Others in Late Modernity*, 2013.
Jabri, V., "Disarming Norms: Postcolonial Aagency and the Constitution of the International", *International Theory*, 6 (2014), 372–390.
Jabri, V./O'gorman, E. (eds.), *Women, Culture, and International Relations*, Boulder, CO 1999.
Jervis, R./Lebow, R. N./Stein, J. G., *Psychology and Deterrence*, Baltimore 1985.
Katzenstein, P. J. (ed.), *The Culture of National Security: Norms and Identity in World Politics*, 1996.
Krishna, S., *Postcolonial Insecurities: India, Sri Lanka, and the Question of Nationhood*, Minneapolis, MN 1999.
Krishna, S., "Race, Amnesia, and the Education of International Relations", *Alternatives: Global, Local, Political*, 26 (2001), 401–424.
Krishna, S. "The Social Life of a Bomb: India and the Ontology of an 'Overpopulated' Society", in Abraham, I. (ed.), *South Asian Cultures of the Bomb: Atomic Publics and the State in India and Pakistan*, 2009, 68–88.
Lee-Koo, K., "Security as Enslavement, Security as Emancipation: Gendered Legacies and Feminist Futures in the Asia-Pacific", in Burke, A./Mcdonald, M. (eds.), *Critical Security in the Asia-Pacific*, Manchester 2007, 231–246.
Loomba, A., *Colonialism/Postcolonialism*, London 2005.
Mamdani, M., *Citizen and Subject : Contemporary Africa and the Legacy of Late Colonialism*, Princeton, N.J. 1996.
Mamdani, M., "Beyond Settler and Native as Political Identities: Ovrcoming the Political Legacy of Colonialism", *Comparative Study of Society and History*, (2001), 651–664.
Mcsweeney, B., *Security, Identity and Interests: A Sociology of International Relations*, Cambridge 1999.
Mignolo, W. D., "The Role of BRICS Countries in the Becoming World Order: 'Humanity', Imperial/Colonial Difference and the Racial Distribution of

Capital and Knoweldge", *Humanity and Difference in the Global Age*, Paris and Brazil: 2012, 41–89.

Mitzen, J., "Ontological Security in World Politics: State Identity and the Security Dilemma", *European Journal of International Relations*, 12 (2006), 341–370.

Muppidi, H., "Postcoloniality and the Production of International Insecurity: The Persistent Puzzle of US-Indian Relations", in Weldes, J./Laffey, M./Gusterson, H./Duvall, R. (eds.), *Cultures of Insecurity: States, Communities, and the Production of Danger*, 1999, 119–146.

Neumann, I. B., *Uses of the Other: 'the East' in European Identity Formation*, Minneapolis 1999.

Neumann, I. B., "Entry Into International Society Reconceptualised: the Case of Russia", *Review of International Studies*, 37 (2011), 463–484.

Pasha, M. K., "Fractured Worlds: Islam, Identity and International Relations", *Global Society*, 17 (2003), 111–120.

Pasha, M. K., "Liberalism, Islam, and International Relations", in Jones, B. G. (ed.), *Decolonizing International Relations*, Lanham 2006, 65–85.

Pasha, M. K., "Untimely Reflections", in Shilliam, R. (ed.), *International Relations and Non-western Thought : Imperialism, Colonialism, and Investigations of Global Modernity.* ilton Park, Abingdon, Oxon, England, New York 2011, 217–226.

Pasha, M. K./Murphy, C. N., "Knowledge/Power/Inequality", *International Studies Review*, 4 (2002), 1–6.

Rumelili, B., *Conflict Resolution and Ontological Security : Peace Anxieties*, London, New York 2015.

Sagan, Scott D., "Why Do States Build Nuclear Weapons?: Three Models in Search of a Bomb", *International Security*, 21: 3 (1996), 54–86.

Said, E. W., *Orientalism*, London 1978.

Said, E. W., *The question of Palestine*, New York 1979.

Said, E. W., *Culture and Imperialism*, New York 1993.

Said, E. W., *The politics of dispossession : the struggle for Palestinian self-determination, 1969–1994*, New York 1994.

Said, E. W., "Secular Interpretation, The Geographical Element and the Methodology of Imperialism", in Prakash, G. (ed.), *After Colonialism: Imperial Histories and Postcolonial Dsiplacements*, Princeton, NJ 1995, 21–39.

Schwarzenberger, G., "The Standard of Civilisation in International Law", *Current legal problems*, 8 (1955), 212–234.

Seth, S. (ed.), *Postcolonial Theory and International Relations: A Critical Introduction*, London 2013.

Shilliam, R., "What the Haitian Revolution Might Tell us About Development, Security, and the Politics of Race", *Comparative Studies in Society and History*, 50 (2008), 778–808.

Stein, J. G., "Threat Perception in International Relations", in Huddy, L./Sears, D. O./Levy, J. S. (eds.), *The Oxford Handbook of Political Psychology*, 2nd ed, Oxford 2013, http://dx.doi.org/10.1093/oxfordhb/9780199760107.013.0012.

Suzuki, S., "Japan's Socialization into Janus-Faced European International Society", *European Journal of International Relations*, 11 (2005), 137–164.

Suzuki, S./Zhang, Y./Quirk, J., "Introduction: The Rest and the Rise of the West", in Suzuki, S./Zhang, Y./Quirk, J. (eds.), *International Orders in the Early Modern World: Before the Rise of the West*, London 2014, 1–11.

Sylvester, C., "Tensions in Feminist Security Studies", *Security Dialogue*, 41 (2010), 607–614.

Tickner, A. B./Wæver, O. (eds.), *Global Scholarship in International Relations: Worlding Beyond the West*, London 2009.

Tickner, J. A., *Gender in International Relations: Feminist Perspectives on Achieving Global Security*, New York, NY 1992.

Vitalis, R., "Birth of a Discipline", in Long, D./Schmidt, B. C. (eds.), *Imperialism and Internationalism in the Discipline of International Relations*. Albany 2005, 159–181.

Walby, S., *Globalization and Inequalities : Complexities and Contested Modernities*, Los Angeles 2009.

Walker, R. B. J., *Inside/outside: International Relations as Political Theory*, Cambridge 1993.

Walker, R. B. J., "International/Inequality", *International Studies Review*, 4 (2002), 7–24.

Watson, A., *The Evolution of International Society : a Comparative Historical Analysis*, London, New York 1992.

Weber, C., *International Relations Theory: A Critical Introduction*, 2010.

Weldes, J./Laffey, M./Gusterson, H./Duvall, R. E., *Cultures of Insecurity: States, Communities and the Production of Danger*, Minneapolis 1999.

Wendt, A./Friedheim, D., Hierarchy Under Anarchy: Informal Empire and the East German State, *International Organization*, 49 (1995), 689–721.

Seeing Culture in World Politics

Christian Reus-Smit

Anxiety about the future of international order is rife: anxiety about the underlying balance of power, anxiety about its economic foundations, anxiety about the corrosive effects of transnationalism, anxiety about the decline of the 'West', and anxiety about any number of other destabilizing challenges. Permeating all of these, however, is an angst about culture, particularly cultural diversity. Concerns about the shifting balance of power are not just about the instability and conflict that often attends power transitions: they are about the rise of non-Western powers that might seek an international order that better reflects their distinctive values and practices. Concerns about the future of global economic governance are not simply about contending state interests: they are about the rise of a global South said to be only tenuously committed to the liberal principles that have so far structured management of the world economy. And while transnationalism has many faces, not the least in the economic realm, it is the intersection between transnationalism and militant religion that fuels anxiety.

In this respect, anxiety about the impact of cultural diversity on the modern international order is the *grund* anxiety of early twenty-first century world politics: it underlies, accentuates, and amplifies a host of other anxieties. Yet like most anxieties, anxiety about cultural diversity is compounded, if not generated, by partial, fragmented, and distorted knowledge: about the nature of culture, about axes of cultural difference, and about the relationship between cultural diversity and political order. For a field claiming unique insights into the nature and development of international order, this knowledge gap is especially pronounced in International Relations (IR). Our understanding is handicapped by varied forms of essentialism, disaggregation, or denial, and despite our trademark willingness to cherry pick insights from diverse disciplines, such as economics and international law, our writings on cultural diversity and international order confidently disregard crucial insights from anthropology, cultural studies, sociology, and history.

This chapter critically examines debate in IR on the relationship between cultural diversity and international order, identifies key insights from anthropology, sociology, and history, and sets out four axioms for future research. After dispensing with some preliminary definitional issues, I introduce two findings from recent research other disciplines: that culture is always highly variegated, often contradictory, and loosely integrated; and that international orders have historically emerged in highly diverse cultural contexts. The chapter then considers four approaches in IR that fail to see culture, including approaches that focus explicitly on cultural phenomena such as norms. In the light of this discussion, the final section sets out four axioms—analytical rules of thumb—for future research on cultural diversity and international order.

Key Concepts

Despite their common usage in both academic and public discourse the concepts of 'culture' and 'international order' are far from settled. Culture, as Raymond Williams observed, "is one of the two or three most complicated words in the English language"[1], and anthropologists, cultural theorists, and sociologists still debate its meaning. I make no attempt here to resolve these debates, but begin instead with a working definition that draws together some of the salient elements of what we might term 'culture'. Culture consists, I suggest, of social meanings embedded in, and expressed through, language, images, bodies, and practices, and these meanings have both constitutive and instrumental effects. As we shall see, any attempt to speak of 'cultures' as discrete, coherent entities is fraught with difficulty, as all cultural formations are highly variegated and contested, only loosely bounded, and deeply interpenetrated. Cultural unity is always more a political project than a fact.

The concept of international order is less contested than that of culture, but it too is subject to varied academic definition and public usage. Hedley Bull famously defined an international order as a purposive arrangement of sovereign states, with preservation of the society of states, territorial independence, and limiting violence being its principal purposes, and

---

1 Williams, *Keywords*, 84.

institutional practices, such as diplomacy and international law, defining its arrangement.[2] This understanding is echoed in John Ikenberry's writings, where international orders are also defined as "the settled rules and arrangements that guide the relations among states"[3]. While this conception captures key aspects of international orders, its analytical value is hampered by its narrowness. The 'arrangement' of an international order is not only, or even primarily, about the external institutional practices that shape relations among sovereign states. As John Ruggie argued three decades ago, the most fundamental aspect of how any international order is arranged concerns how its constituent units are differentiated from one another: how they are "separated and segmented"[4]. International orders differ markedly in the nature of such differentiation: in some, like the modern order, units are differentiated on the principle of sovereignty, but in others the structuring principles have been empire, suzerainty or heteronomy. Given this, my preference is to define international orders more broadly than Bull and Ikenberry, thus accommodating differently arranged orders, and providing a better framework for thinking about 'systems' change between such orders. International orders are, I propose, systemic configurations of political authority, comprising multiple units of political authority, separated according to some principle of differentiation.[5]

Insights from Elsewhere

Most IR scholars have nothing to say about culture, and only marginally more about changes in international orders. The causal significance of culture is generally discounted in favour of interests and power, and if scholars are interested in international change, it is systemic not systems change that concerns them.[6] Among those who are interested in culture and international order, however, the overwhelming tendency is to

---

2 Bull, *The Anarchical Society*, Chap. 1.
3 Ikenberry, *After Victory*, 47.
4 Ruggie, Continuity and Transformation, 274.
5 For a more extended discussion, see Reus-Smit, The Liberal International Order.
6 Systemic change is change within an existing international system—a shift in the balance of power, for example—and systems change is change from one system, or order, to another. See Gilpin, *War and Change*.

essentialize culture and exaggerate its causal significance. There are two versions of this. For some, international orders emerge out of unitary cultural contexts, and their survival and stability depend on the robustness of these cultural foundations. In a position emblematic of early English School thinking, Martin Wight wrote that "a states system will not come into being without a degree of cultural unity among its members", and he worried that as post-1945 decolonization brought more non-Western states into the system that the modern order had "outrun cultural and moral community"[7]. For others, great powers are thickly constituted cultural actors, embodying a single, coherent culture, and destined to enact deeply etched cultural scripts. Martin Jacques' *When China Rules the World* is a good example of this.[8] Samuel Huntington's *Clash of Civilizations* brought together these two versions: the modern international order was rooted in Western civilization, he famously argued, and the rise of culturally driven, non-Western powers heralded its demise.[9]

For specialists in the study of culture, such views are curious to say the least, conjuring on to the stage long discredited 1930s understandings of culture and its effects. Anthropologists, cultural theorists, and sociologists no longer think of cultures as coherent things. It is axiomatic today that cultural formations are variegated, contradictory, and contested, that they are loosely integrated and lack clear boundaries, and that they are mutually interpenetrated and constituted. IR scholars frequently cite Ann Swidler's argument that culture is like a tool kit, that actors select norms, principles, and practices in the strategic pursuit of their interests. They miss, however, her more fundamental point: that "all real cultures contain diverse, often conflicting symbols, rituals, stories, and guides to action"[10]. So important is this insight that some anthropologists have called for a focus on the organization of cultural diversity, not culture *per se*.[11] Unlike their counterparts in IR, political theorists interested in multiculturalism were quick to enlist these new understandings. James Tully famously labeled culture a "strange multiplicity" characterized by a "tangled labyrinth of intertwining cultural differences *and* similarities"[12]. More recently, in a major new work on

---

7 Wight, *Systems of States*, 22, 33; Bull had a similar view. See Bull, *The Anarchical Society*, 16, 317.
8 Jacques, *When China Rules*.
9 Huntington, *The Clash of Civilization*.
10 Swidler, Culture in Action, 277.
11 Hannerz, Diversity.
12 Tully, *Strange Multiplicity*, 11.

minority rights, Alan Patten argues that "In groups of any size, beliefs and practices are heterogeneous and contested. They change and fluctuate over time. And they are formed interactively and dialogically with members of other groups, often taking on a recognizably hybrid character as a result"[13].

This shift to seeing culture as inherently diverse has raised questions about what gives culture any kind of form, above and beyond its constituent meanings and practices. A prominent answer appeals to social institutions. Institutions are, of course, cultural artifacts themselves, reflecting and expressing a society's deeper norms, values, and practices. But once they exist, once they constitute social facts, they condition the 'flow' of culture, accentuating or suppressing, structuring and channeling, and reproducing or reconstituting meanings and practices. In Ulf Hannerz' words, "In the continuous interdependence of "the social" and "the cultural" [...] the social structure of persons and relationships channels the cultural flow at the same time as it is being, in part, culturally produced"[14]. This emphasis on the role of social institutions is a central theme of Swidler's later work on the sociology of love[15], and features prominently in recent research on multiculturalism and racial justice. Kenan Malik shows, for example, how institutional practices take complex heterogeneity and construct authorized forms of diversity, "putting people into ethnic and cultural boxes [...] and defining there needs and rights accordingly"[16].

If all of this is true, and we have little reason to believe it isn't, then it was only a matter of time before a new generation of industrious historians would discover that international orders seldom if ever grow out of unitary cultural contexts—how could they if there is no such thing as a unitary culture? A wave of new histories now shows not only that international orders generally emerge in heterogeneous cultural environments, but that the management, or governance, of diversity has been a key imperative of order-building. The early modern European order (1520–1750)[17] developed out of the cultural ferment of the Protestant Reformation, the Qing Chinese order (1644–1911) was characterized by "intertwined cultural diversity"[18], and the Ottoman order (1299-1908) "was not just

---

13 Patten, *Equal Recognition*, 40.
14 Hannerz, Diversity, 14.
15 Swidler, *Talk of Love*.
16 Malik, The Failure of Multiculturalism, 21f.; also see Berrey, *The Enigma of Diversity*.
17 Cameron, *The European Reformation*.
18 Shiyuan, Ethnicities, 91.

Ottoman, Turkish, or Islamic. It was all of these combined with Roman and Byzantine, Balkan, and Turco-Mongol institutions and practices"[19]. In all of these, institutions were constructed to order and manage diversity. In early modern Europe sovereignty was in part a solution to the problem of religious difference.[20] In Qing China the Lifanyuan system evolved to govern minorities. And in the Ottoman case, the Janissary and Millet systems governed relations between Muslims, Christians, and Jews.[21]

Four Paths to Blindness

I have already noted that many IR scholars have little if anything to say about culture, but I want to push this claim one step further. I want to suggest that cultural blindness is a feature of all of our major theories, even those explicitly concerned with cultural phenomena. This will sound odd indeed, especially since I have just highlighted approaches to international order that essentialize culture and exaggerate its effects. There are different ways of 'not seeing', however. A theory can be blind to culture because culture has no place in its ontology: its assumptions about the nature of the international political universe do not include culture as a causally significant element. Heavily materialist versions of realism exhibit such blindness. But blindness can also take a second form. A theory can be blind to culture by not seeing it for what it is: by looking but not seeing. This is the blindness of the essentialist approaches to international order discussed above, but it is also characteristic of much constructivism, and of rationalist approaches that seek to accommodate culture.

When I say that a theory can be blind by not seeing culture for what it is, I am not suggesting that there is a Platonic form of culture that can be known objectively, and that all one needs to attain such truth is a correct conception of culture. Nowhere more than in the study of culture do the core interpretivist axioms apply: that our immersion in the social universe we observe makes our knowledge inherently subjective, and that our understandings are always mediated by our concepts. It is not unreasonable to suggest, however, that viewing the world through a conception of a

---

19 Barkey, *Empire of Difference*, 8.
20 For a good statement of this position see Jackson, The Global Covenant, 181.
21 See Ning, *Lifanyuan and the Management*; Barkey 2008.

culture that is stubbornly at odds with the understandings of specialist disciplines, and radically inconsistent with everything we know empirically about culture's complexities, amounts to a form of blindness.

Ontologically Irrelevant

Realism is the most straightforward, least interesting, and easily dispensed with example of cultural blindness. Most realist theories in IR have two key characteristics: they are materialist, and they are statist. Both are ontological commitments. In the realist world view the stuff that matters, the stuff that drives international relations, is material: the distribution of material capabilities at the structural level, and material interests—guns and money—at the unit level. Realists do not deny the existence of non-material things in world politics, such as norms, rules, and principles, only that they have any causal significance. Sometimes this is because they are epiphenomena, sometimes because they are nothing more than tools of the powerful, and sometimes because they lie outside the causal chain altogether. Lacking any causal relevance, non-material things such as these lie outside the realist line of sight: when they look at international relations, this is simply not what they see.

The other realist ontological commitment is statism. This is not just that realists think sovereign states are the most important actors—which they do—it is that the international system, the dynamics of which they seek to understand, is a system *of* states. As Alexander Wendt observed, states are 'primitive' in realist theory: the very notion of an international system—its anarchical structure and attendant dynamics—presupposes the existence of states. How this contributes to realism's cultural blindness is more complicated though than the role of materialism. As noted above, realists do not generally see states as cultural actors; they see them as driven by material interests. But when on the rare occasion that they take a cultural turn, as Huntington so famously did, their statism frames how they understand culture. The need to see states as coherent actors with clearly identifiable interests, and the associated impulse to bracket the complexities and contradictions of domestic social and political life, lead to the nationalization and essentializing of culture. States become cultural billiard balls, with culture neatly bounded by the state's territorial frontiers, cultural conflicts and contradictions homogenized away, and foreign policy imagined as a cultural script, more or less enabled by available material power.

Essentialized out of Existence

If realists bracket culture as ontologically irrelevant, only to essentialize it when belatedly discovered, another, increasingly prominent perspective, makes culture ontologically primary. As noted above, this is especially pronounced among those interesting in the relationship between culture and international order. It is particularly problematic, therefore, that the view of culture expressed here is so markedly inconsistent with current thinking in anthropology, cultural theory, sociology, and history.

As noted above, this perspective on culture and international order has been most clearly and consistently articulated by key figures of the English School. In stark contrast to the current view that cultures are inherently heterogeneous, and that international orders evolve in highly variegated and contested cultural contexts, these figures understood cultures as singular and coherent, and political orders, domestic and international, as dependent on such foundations. Adda Bozeman provided a particularly succinct articulation of this conception: "Cultures are different", she wrote,

"because they are associated with different modes of thought. [...] The successive generations of any given society will be inclined to think in traditionally preferred groves, to congregate around certain constant, change-resistant themes, and to rebut, whether intentionally or unconsciously, contrary ideas intruding from without."[22]

The importance of culture, so defined, to the development of international orders was stressed not only by Wight but also Hedley Bull. In a key passage in *The Anarchical Society*, he wrote that a common culture enables "the definition of common rules and the evolution of common institutions with a sense of common values"[23]. Understanding culture and its impact on international order in these ways generated profound concerns among English School writers about the future of order in the multicultural world of post-1945 decolonization. Bozeman was especially pessimistic: There is a profound gap, she wrote, "between the inner normative orders of the

---

22 Bozeman, *The Future of Law*, 14.
23 Bull, *The Anarchical Society*, 16.

vast majority of states on the on hand, and the substantive concepts of established international law and organization on the other"[24]. Bull was more optimistic, but argued that the future of the modern order would "be determined [...] by the preservation and extension of a cosmopolitan culture that can provide the world international society of today with the kind of underpinning enjoyed by the geographically smaller and more culturally homogeneous international societies of the past"[25].

Far from just the outmoded thinking of long dead members of the English School, these views find expression in much of today's commentary about the future of international order. In his 2014 speech to the UN Security Council, President Obama told delegates that

"we come together as United Nations with a choice to make. We can renew the international system that has enabled so much progress, or we can allow ourselves to be pulled back into the undertow of instability. [...] And it is no exaggeration to say that humanity's future depends on us uniting against those who would divide us along the fault lines of tribe, sect, race, or religion."[26]

Henry Kissinger, in his recent book *World Order*, poses this as one of the key questions of contemporary international relations: "Can regions with such diverse cultures, histories, and traditional theories of order vindicate the legitimacy of any common system"[27]. Writing in the *New Statesman*, Kevin Rudd, the former Australian Prime Minister, posed the issue in this way:

"Very soon we will find ourselves at a point in history when, for the first time since George III, a non-Western, non-democratic state will be the largest economy in the world. If this is the case, how will China exercise its power in the future international order? Will it accept the culture, norms and structure of the postwar order? Or will China seek to change it?"[28]

Each of these examples assumes that the modern international order had Western cultural foundations, and that cultural diversity, intersecting with new configurations of power, threatens fragmentation and conflict.

From the perspective of contemporary scholarship and research, however, it is not clear that culture, in any real sense, features in these accounts.

---

24 Bozeman, *The Future of Law*, 181.
25 Bull, *The Anarchical Society*, 317.
26 Obama, *President Barack Obama*.
27 Kissinger, *World Order*, 8.
28 Rudd, The West Isn't Ready.

Nowhere are the complexities and contradictions of culture admitted let alone analyzed, and nowhere is the politics of culture that attended the development of any actual international orders acknowledged. Instead culture takes the stage as the most simplistic of analytical devices: a homogeneous system of neatly integrated and bounded norms, values, and practices that together have a primary, uncomplicated causal impact on the nature and stability of international orders. Cultural diversity is, in turn, understood in equally simplistic terms. Diversity, in such accounts, is nothing more than an absence—the absence of cultural unity—and it is assumed to have only one effect: the destabilization and erosion of order. It is never entertained, let alone acknowledged, that cultural diversity might, in some registers and contexts, have a generative impact on the development of international orders, which has in fact been the case. And when diversity is discussed at the international level, cultural essentialism is reproduced at the unit level. Cultural diversity is now seen as a problem for world order, but China, whose rise is the source of much of this anxiety, is treated as a coherent cultural entity, a 'civilizational state' in Martin Jacques' words.

Disaggregated to Bits

The idea that cultural phenomena are ontologically primary is also found in constructivism, which sees norms, rules, and principles as not just regulatory, but also constitutive. These intersubjective meanings, as Jepperson, Wendt, and Katzenstein explained in *The Culture of National Security*,

"either define ("constitute") identities in the first place (generating expectations about the proper portfolio of identities for a given context) or prescribe or proscribe ("regulate") behaviors for already constituted identities (generating expectations about how those identities will shape behavior in varying circumstances)"[29].

But while constructivists are at one with the English School in seeing norms as constitutive, as shaping actors identities and interests in given contexts, they lack the homogenizing impulse of Wight, Bull, and Bozeman. For the latter, culture is an order-wide, integrated system of

---

29 Jepperson, Wendt and Katzenstein, Norms, Identity, and Culture, 54.

meaning, but for constructivists culture has little presence beyond individual norms.

To be sure, early constructivists used the term 'culture' liberally. For example, my own book on the origins of fundamental institutions was titled *The Moral Purpose of the State: <u>Culture</u>, Social Identity, and Institutional Rationality in International Relations*[30]. But like most constructivist works that invoked the concept in this way, culture quickly disappears, replaced by a focus on individual norms, or discrete sets of such norms. Indeed, constructivism quickly became associated, somewhat narrowly in my mind, with the study of individual norms, and many of its pioneering works took this form: Audie Klotz on anti-racist norms, Martha Finnemore on norms of non-intervention, Richard Price on the chemical weapons taboo, Reus-Smit on constitutional norms, Kathryn Sikkink on human rights norms, Nina Tannenwald on the norm against the use of nuclear weapons, the list goes on. In seeking to understand such norms, constructivists soon found they needed to talk about relationships between individual norms, but this has usually been highly circumscribed, focusing narrowly on dyadic or triadic relations among norms. This is where they honed the notions of nesting and grafting, in which communicative action theories are invoked to show how the construction of norm B is discursively dependent on the prior acceptance of norm A. In my own work, issue-specific norms were seen as dependent on fundamental institutional norms, which were in turn dependent on even deeper constitutional norms.

One virtue of constructivism is that it avoids homogenizing culture. By focusing on individual norms, and building up no further than dyadic or triadic relationships, constructivists are, by default, treating culture as heterogeneous, even normatively fragmented. However, this virtue is an unintended consequence of disaggregation, not the product of any systematic reflection on the nature and implications of cultural diversity. Cultural formations are heterogeneous, loosely integrated, and deeply interpenetrated, but they also exhibit structural features and dynamics, complex processes and practices, and far reaching webs of interconnection. Even their contradictions bind as much as they divide, and cultural struggles can be generative as well as corrosive. Constructivists are blind to these features of culture, and as a consequence, they have little say about how international order might arise in such cultural contexts. In fact, when

---

30 Reus-Smit, *The Moral Purpose*, underline added.

constructivists do consider the development of international orders, they replicate their standard approach to the study of norms, this time focusing on the development of deep, structuring *grund* norms, usually reflecting the prevailing cultural order. At this point, however, constructivists come dangerously close to replicating the essentialism and determinism of the English School. In my own work, although insisting that deep constitutional norms are hegemonic not totalizing, and that counterhegemonic ideas characterize any international society, I focus nonetheless on particular constitutional norms, rooted in broader cultural values and practices, and cognitively and discursively constitutive of a second tier of fundamental institutions.[31]

Nothing but Common Knowledge

Rational-choice theory in IR is regularly dismissed as incapable of comprehending the social or the cultural in world politics. Its methodological individualism—the idea that analytically you start from individual interests and build up—is in fact closer to an ontological individualism, where society is conceived as little more than a market place that atomistic individuals enter as they pursue pre-existing, pre-social interests. Unlike realism, this ontology is not materialist, even if in practice it is often assumed that the interests of utility-maximizing individuals are material. In principle, the preferences individuals pursue in the social market place can take any form: they could be egoistic and material, but also other-regarding and normative. Nonetheless, the very focus on individual preferences is often considered sufficient to discount rationalism in the study of culture and international relations.

Yet few rationalists would go as far as Margaret Thatcher in claiming that 'there is no such thing as society'. Not only do they acknowledge an intersubjective realm above and beyond atomistic individuals and their preferences—international regimes, for example—they have increasingly sought to accommodate more specifically cultural phenomena, such as symbols and rituals. The problem is not a lack of interest, therefore. Rather, it is that rationalists seek to integrate culture within modified

---

31 Ibid., Chap. 2.

choice-theoretic models, and this encourages a particular understanding of the nature and effects of culture.

It is worth recalling here the logical structure of IR's most prominent rationalist thesis: neoliberal institutionalism. States are imagined as atomistic, utility-maximizers; to realize their interests they have to solve coordination and collaboration problems generated by anarchy; and to do this they create international regimes: norms, rules, and decision-making processes that increase information, lower transaction costs, and deter cheating. Rationalist attempts to integrate culture follow this basic logic, though in considerably more sophisticated form. Two examples illustrate this.

In *Rational Ritual*, Michael Chwe argues that in order to solve coordination problems—problems that arise when "each person wants to participate in a group action but only if others also want to participate"— individuals need common knowledge.[32] An "event or fact is common knowledge among a group of people if everyone knows it, everyone knows that everyone knows it, and everyone knows that everyone knows that everyone knows it, and so on"[33]. In the same way that regimes in neoliberal theory increase information, it is cultural practices, according to Chwe, that help generate common knowledge. Cultural rituals play a particularly important role here: "A public ritual is not just about the transmission of meaning; it is also about letting audience members know that other audience members know"[34]. Where most interpretations concentrate on the meanings embedded in rituals, Chwe argues that they "must also be understood in terms of publicity or, more precisely, common knowledge generation"[35].

In *Honor, Symbols, and War*, Barry O'Neill focuses less on collaboration problems than on the recurrent conflicts and tensions characterizing world politics. Many of these are generated by symbolic politics, which he claims is just as amenable to strategic analysis as "resources, interests, and power"[36]. Political leaders, he contends, have an abiding interest in 'status regulators': they "worry about intangible goals like saving face and preserving national honor and prestige," and their pursuit of these goals

---

[32] Chwe, *Rational Ritual*, 3.
[33] Ibid., 9f.
[34] Ibid., 4.
[35] Ibid., 15.
[36] O'Neill, *Honor*, xii.

often generates conflicts, even if success depends on social recognition.[37] Focusing on four such regulators—honor, social face, prestige, and moral authority—O'Neill shows how they depend on three kinds of symbols: value, message, and focal symbols. Here is not the place for a detailed account of these regulators or symbols. It is sufficient to observe that in O'Neill's account the regulators depend on common knowledge, and the symbols, like Chwe's rituals, play a key role in generating such knowledge. For example, "[s]ocial face is the group's expectation about how it will treat the individual in direct interactions", and "[p]restige is the belief among the members that the person is admired—each one's belief that the rest of the group believes that the individual possesses the desirable trait"[38]. To maintain social face and enhance prestige, political leaders manipulate symbols, a primary purpose of which is the construction of common knowledge. "Focal symbols", for example, "are events, often not deliberate acts by any agent, that induce observers to adopt a common judgment about what move they will they will make in an important situation"[39].

It may well be the case that rituals can provide the common knowledge needed to solve collaboration problems, and it may be true that actors manipulate symbols to enhance their status, but like our previous perspectives, rationalism is blind to key aspects of culture, aspects central to any understanding of the relationship between cultural diversity and international order. To begin with, the constitutive effects of culture lie outside its gaze. Actors clearly use symbols and rituals instrumentally, and consciously so. But they are also cultural products: their identities and interests conditioned by their lived cultural norms and practices. Essentialists simplify and exaggerate this dimension of culture; rationalists ignore it. Second, like constructivism, rationalism has the virtue of not homogenizing culture. Because they focus on utility-maximizers using rituals to build common knowledge, or manipulating symbols to enhance their status, the cultural universe is little more than the sum total of strategically useful cultural phenomena. But like constructivism, this comes at a cost. Cultural formations may not be homogeneous, but even the most diverse have structural features and effects, as well as complex, intertwined processes and practices. Rationalist models have little purchase on this

---

37 Ibid., xi.
38 Ibid., xii.
39 Ibid.

broader cultural terrain. Finally, while cultural phenomena may help build common knowledge, it is not at all clear that this is the only reason they exist, or the only role they perform. Furthermore, if we stand back and consider cultural formations more broadly, the knowledge generated by their multiplicity of meanings and practices is likely to be as varied and contradictory as the phenomena themselves. And, as Hannerz, Swidler, and others argue, it may be social institutions that bring some form to this diversity.

Where to From Here?

Understanding how cultural diversity affects international order is a critical contemporary challenge. But as we have seen, IR scholars face this challenge with have an impoverished understanding of culture: it is either off their ontological radars, or what they see is radically out of sync with current understandings in anthropology, cultural theory, sociology, and history. In this final section I propose four correctives; conceptual and analytical propositions that build on key insights from other disciplines, and together provide a more fruitful starting point for understanding the impact of new articulations of cultural difference, and axes of cultural diversity, have on the future of the modern international order.

Diversity is the Norm, Unity is a Project

Taking culture seriously demands recognition of its inherent diversity, and the only way to avoid the traps of essentialism is to assume such diversity from the outset. This is the reverse of how IR scholars currently 'take culture seriously', where they either start by assuming unity—the unity of national cultures, or the unity of an orders' cultural foundations—or they disaggregate culture into normative fragments, ignoring the organization of diversity (more on this below). If we accept how specialist disciplines now understand culture, we should place unity in question. We should assume, as an analytical starting point, that cultural unity is almost always a political project (for better or worse), and that evidence of unity is an accomplishment of human practices—practices in need of explanation.

Any attempt to take cultural diversity seriously has to withstand what I shall call 'the trap of aggregation'. Presently, when IR scholars think about cultural diversity—when they worry about the impact of diversity on the stability of political orders, for example—they imagine diversity as the multiplicity of discrete and coherent cultural units: ethnic groups, nations, civilizations. This perspective aggregates culture into homogeneous cultural units, and locates diversity in the spaces between such units. We know, however, that such aggregated units are myths. In reality, ethnicities, nationalities, and civilizations are riddled with, and entwined within, complex forms and expressions of diversity—diversity political elites commonly deny, even actively suppress.

One way to avoid the trap of aggregation is to focus on axes of cultural diversity that do not presuppose mythologized cultural units. Existing literatures suggest four such axes: meaning complexity, diversity of interpretation, identity pluralism, and multiple identities.

If cultural formations are systems of meaning, expressed through symbols and practices, they are highly complex systems, characterized by a myriad of meanings, some mutually reinforcing, others deeply contradictory. Individuals do not experience their cultural environments as singular, seamless wholes: our environments send mixed messages. Within the state, the meanings mobilized in the service of national unity coexist, often uncomfortably, with contrasting cosmopolitan, regional, ethnic, class, and gendered meanings, and cross-cutting political cultural meanings frequently betray markedly different conceptions of the scope and purpose of political authority. Most globalizing societies evince complex mixes of 'traditional' and 'modern' cultural meanings, generating contestation at multiple levels, from the family to issues of public policy. The fact of meaning complexity is central to Stephen Krasner's oft-quoted critique of the causal significance of norms in world politics. At the global level, multiple, often contradictory norms coexist, allowing leaders to choose norms that serve their strategic interests. The diversity of normative resources undermines the causal power of any particular norm while adding the manipulation of norms for other ends. In world politics, Krasner concludes, "logics of consequences dominate logics of appropriateness"[40].

Just as individuals don't experience cultural environments as singular, seamless wholes, they don't interpret the meanings that enmesh them in

---

40 Krasner, *Sovereignty*, 51.

the same way. Meaning indeterminancy is a feature of all social norms, values, and practices, and individuals read these meanings differently. Scholarship on this is most developed in the field of law, where norms are often formalized and subject to authoritative interpretation. Yet even in this area, it is now axiomatic that the law is inherently indeterminate, with considerable latitude for interpretation. This indeterminacy stems in part from the 'semantic openness of legal speech' (words and phrases can be open to diverse interpretation), and in part from the contradictory reasons that produced this speech in the first place.[41] Beyond the law prominent examples of meaning indeterminacy abound. The great confessional schism that divided Catholics and Protestants in sixteenth century Europe is one example, as is today's divisions among Muslims over the interpretation of the Quran.

Most social orders comprise a plurality of identities, as well as groups that coalesce around these identities. Often these identities are ethnic, racial, religious, linguistic, or historical, but they can take other forms as well: civilizational or rooted in settler/indigenous distinctions, for example. In all cases, these identities are social, in the sense that they are "sets of meanings that an actor attributes to itself while taking into account the perspective of others, that is, as a social object"[42]. Understood in this way, identities fulfill a variety of social-psychological purposes. Most importantly, they provide "primary sources of plans for action"[43], information individuals' actions as well as strategies. Both assimilationist and multicultural policies assume, as their starting point, that a social order comprises a plurality of identities: the former seeks to replace such pluralism with a single national identity; the latter seeks to recognize, even celebrate, it. At the international level, it is the growing plurality of ever more powerful identities that worries many contemporary observers: the identities of non-Western great powers; the identities of transnational religious insurgents.

But if the diversity engendered by the existence of a plurality of identities in any given social order were not enough, this axis of diversity is further complicated by the fact that individuals do not have single identities: they have multiple meaningful identities simultaneously. For example, I identify as an Australian, a Melbournian, a cosmopolitan, an

---

41 Koskenniemi, *From Apology to Utopia*, 590–596.
42 Wendt, Collective Identity Formation, 385.
43 McCall and Simmons, *Identities*, 69.

atheist, a professor, a father, a husband, a runner/cyclist/rower, etc. Individuals move in and out of such identities according to social context, and learn how to narrate, in socially intelligible ways, these fluid complexes of identities. This multiplicity, and its contextual fluidity, has been highly consequential politically. In the sixteenth century, when Europeans encountered the New World they identified as Christians, but when they faced each other in Europe it was as Catholics and Protestants, and increasingly French, English, Spanish, etc. In 1949 East Bengalis joined the new state of Pakistan on the basis of religion, but in 1971 fought for an independent Bangladesh on the basis of their distinct linguistic identity.

Diversity is More Than an Absence of Unity

As noted above, in International Relations cultural diversity is nothing more than an absence, the lack of cultural unity. This is true for essentialists and liberal pluralists. The former assume that international orders emerge out of unitary cultural contexts, and diversity is treated as the withdrawal of a primary ordering mechanism—diversity is a vacuum. For the latter, international institutions—from sovereignty to multilateralism—accommodate actors with diverse backgrounds and values, and thus cultural diversity washes out, requiring no further content or elaboration. But if cultural diversity is an existential background condition of world politics, as I have suggested above, then we need to understand it as more than an absence.

In the previous section I set out four axes of diversity—meaning complexity, diversity of interpretation, identity pluralism, and multiple identities. This implies that diversity is the same as heterogeneity. Indeed, the Oxford English Dictionary defines the latter in terms of the former: heterogeneous means 'diverse in character or content'. I want to suggest, however, that cultural diversity is more than heterogeneity: that in all social orders cultural diversity is patterned and structured, sometimes by design, sometimes as a byproduct of other practices and processes. It is this insight that has prompted some anthropologists to advocate a focus not on culture *per se* but on the organization of diversity, as Hannerz puts it. A fine example of such a focus is Ellen Berrey's recent book *The Enigma of Diversity*, which shows how the adoption of 'diversity' as an organizational value in the United States, has led to a reconfiguration of the prevailing racial order, the 'inequality regime' that "establishes boundaries around groups based on their phenotype or ancestry [...] [and] positions those groups on a hierarchy, and structures their relations to each other"[44].

Seeing diversity as patterned and structured raises two key questions for those of us interested in the relationship between cultural diversity and international order: How is diversity organized in any given order, and what factors have contributed to this organization? The first is empirical and beyond the scope of this chapter. The second is also empirical, at least when asked of any particular order. Yet existing literatures suggest several possible factors. We should assume, at the outset, that the axes of cultural diversity outlined in the previous section have no inherent political implications. When they come to the fore, how they are expressed, and what effects they have will depend on a range of conditioning factors. A 'conditioning factor' is defined here as a structure or practice (material or social) that heightens the political salience of axes of diversity, affecting their visibility, enabling their mobilization, empowering some actors over others, and creating incentives for particular interpretations of cultural difference.

IR theory suggests four possible conditioning factors. For realists, it is axiomatic that the distribution of material capabilities will determine the salience of forms of cultural diversity. When one state within an international order has preponderant material capabilities, it will have the capacity to propagate its own cultural values and practices—material preponderance generates cultural hegemony. Similarly, when material capabilities are distributed diffusely—as in a multipolar international order—forms of cultural diversity are likely to be more salient. Current concerns about the rise of non-Western states rest on the assumed significance of this factor. A second factor is prevailing institutional frameworks, a factor emphasized in recent anthropological and historical work on the organization of diversity.[45] As we have seen, this factor is also privileged in liberal pluralist arguments about the capacity of the modern international order to accommodate states with diverse cultural backgrounds and values.

A third factor is the interaction capacity of a given order. Barry Buzan and Richard Little argue persuasively that the development of international orders is profoundly affected by their interaction capacity, by their

---

44 Berrey, *The Enigma of Diversity*, 15.
45 See Hannerz, *Cultural Complexity*, 14; and Sewell, *Logics of History*, 172–175.

"physical potential for enabling the units to exchange information, goods, or blows"[46]. This factor has featured in recent debates about the impact of cultural diversity on domestic social and political orders. In a widely reported study, Putnam found that in ethnically diverse communities "Trust (even of one's own race) is lower, altruism and community cooperation rarer, friends fewer"[47]. Yet these findings have been challenged by subsequent research that factored in levels of interaction. "A crucial determinant of whether diversity will respond in positive or negative attitudes towards ethnic out-groups," Sturgis et.al. conclude, is the amount of "social contact and interaction between residents"[48]. The final factor is political practices. Actors are both constituted by their cultural environments—their identities, interests, and strategies shaped by cultural norms and values—and they engage creatively with the diverse meanings and practices they encounter. Political actors, in particular, enhance their power and pursue their interests by highlighting some meanings while suppressing others. They ordain some interpretations as authoritative, and utilize these privileged interpretations to craft individual and collective identities, and license desired political projects. Nowhere has this been more comprehensively documented than in studies of nationalism.[49]

Managing Diversity is a Key Imperative of Order Building

In essentialist accounts cultural unity is a constitutive background condition for the construction of international orders, and the institutional architectures of such orders instantiate dominant cultural values and practices. Even in liberal pluralists arguments that see today's institutions as uniquely able to accommodate states and peoples of diverse cultures, it is assumed that these institutions are Western and liberal in origin. Yet Wight's proposition that a "states system will not come into being without a degree of cultural unity among its members" (Wight, *Systems of States*, 33) now appears increasingly at odds with the evidence. As explained earlier, new histories show that pretty well all historical international orders

---

46 Buzan and Little, *International Systems*, 80.
47 Putnam, E Pluribus Unum, 137.
48 Sturgis, Brunton-Smith, Kuha and Jackson, Ethnic Diversity, 4.
49 Anderson, *Imagined Communities*; Gellner, *Nations and Nationalism*; Hobsbawm, *Nations and Nationalism*; and Rae, *State Identities*.

we can think of—the early modern, the Chinese, the Ottoman, etc.—emerged in heterogeneous cultural contexts. Furthermore, all of these orders developed institutions to manage diversity. The early modern international order, long seen as a child of Latin Christendom, is now understood to have been deeply conditioned by cultural encounters with Islam and the New World, and by the profound religious schism of the Reformation. Territorial sovereignty, and then institutionalized practices of inclusion and exclusion infused with ideas of civilizational hierarchy, evolved in significant measure to construct and discipline diversity in particular ways.

That international orders evolve in part to manage existential cultural diversity is not only historically apparent, but also theoretically explicable. International orders, like all systems of rule, depend for their stability not only on material power, but on legitimacy. In contexts characterized, first, by an uneven distribution of material capabilities, and second, by cultural diversity, legitimacy depends on transformation material power into political authority, and diversity into ordered patterns of cultural recognition. The former involves the definition of units of legitimate political authority, and how they stand in relation to one another; the second involves defining legitimate axes of cultural difference, and ordering these normatively. For example, in early modern Europe the political units were emergent sovereign states, and the privileged axis of cultural difference was religion (as opposed to civilization or nation, for example). Both of these are acts of power, as both establish patterns of inclusion and exclusion, and both generate social and political hierarchies.

In essentialist accounts, echoed in much of the anxiety about current transformations in international order, cultural diversity has only one effect: the erosion of order. But if we understand it the way I propose here, then cultural diversity has also been generative of order. Berrey distinguishes between diversity as heterogeneity, and diversity as organizational ideal.[50] In the development of international orders, diversity works at both levels: diversity (qua heterogeneity) is an existential condition out of which orders develop; and diversity (as an organizational ideal) informs practices of recognition and licenses the construction of particular institutional architectures.

---

50 Berrey, *The Enigma of Diversity*, 25–27.

Systems Change Always Entails Shifts in Diversity Regimes

IR scholars commonly distinguish between systems and systemic change: the former change from one system to another (medieval heteronomy to a sovereign state system, for example), the latter change within a system (commonly a shift in polarity).[51] Elsewhere I argued that systems change can be either configurative or purposive. Configurative change occurs when there is a change in organizing principle, say from heteronomy to sovereignty. Purposive change can occur with or without configurative change, and entails a shift in the underlying norms governing political legitimacy, norms I term the *moral purpose of the state*[52]. The shift from Europe's Absolutist order to the modern liberal order was just such a shift.

The arguments about cultural diversity canvassed in this chapter suggest an important addition or revision to this understanding of change. If all international orders emerge in heterogeneous cultural contexts, and if all develop institutions to manage diversity, then systems change, whether configurative or purposive, will necessarily involve a shift from one diversity regime to another. We can think about the change from Europe's heteronomous order to Absolutism in this way, and so too the shift from Absolutism to the modern order. Most importantly, this challenges the questions we ask of contemporary transformations. For essentialists, the central question is how the Western order can survive the rise of non-Western powers. From the perspective advanced here, the key question is whether the diversity regime that emerged within the modern order can accommodate new conjunctions of material power and articulations of cultural difference. Only by understanding the nature of this regime, its adaptive capacities, and the nature of new conjunctions of power and difference can we answer this question.

Conclusion

Present anxieties about the impact of cultural diversity on the future of the modern international order are founded on assumptions about culture and order that are radically inconsistent with thinking in specialist disciplines

---

51 The classic statement is provided by Gilpin, *War and Change*.
52 Reus-Smit, *The Moral Purpose*, 162–165.

such as anthropology, sociology, and history. But the obverse reaction in IR, which denies culture any causal significance in world politics, is equally unsustainable. It asks us to discount entirely the cultural dimensions of key contemporary transformations, particularly the rise of non-Western great powers and transnational religious insurgencies, as well as landmark historical phenomena, such as the impact of the Wars of Religion on the early-modern order, the role of civilizational hierarchies in 19th century imperialism, and the impact of liberal values on post-1945 international institutions.

This chapter suggests a way forward, a new way of seeing culture in world politics. I began with key insights from history and the cultural 'sciences', and then showed how existing approaches to culture in IR— from the strongly essentialist to the strongly rationalist—are blind to culture (as it is currently understood). To understand the relationship between cultural diversity and international order we have to stop seeing diversity a new emerged challenge to order, and take it as our starting point. This means not only treating cultural diversity as the existential condition in which all orders emerge, but as more than an absence of unity. We need to see diversity as distinct from heterogeneity; we need to see it as patterned and structured, and then ask what factors, in any given context, serve to organize diversity. The modern international order organizes diversity in a particular way—it has a distinct diversity regime—and the question today is how new conjunctions of material power and articulations of cultural difference challenge this regime, and with what implications.

References

Anderson, B, *Imagined Communities*, Rev. Ed., London 2006.
Barkey, K., *Empire of Difference: The Ottomans in Comparative Perspective*, Cambridge 2008.
Berrey, E., *The Enigma of Diversity: The Language of Race and the Limits of Racial Justice*, Chicago 2015.
Bozeman, A., *The Future of Law in a Multicultural World*, Princeton NJ 1971.
Bull, H., *The Anarchical Society*, 2nd ed., London 1999.
Buzan, B./Little, R., *International Systems in World History*, Oxford, 2000.
Cameron, E., *The European Reformation*, 2nd ed., Oxford 2012.

Chwe, M. S.-Y., *Rational Ritual: Culture, Coordination, and Common Knowledge*, Princeton NJ 2001.
Gellner, E, *Nations and Nationalism*, 2nd ed., Ithaca 2009.
Gilpin, R., *War and Change in World Politics*, Cambridge 1981.
Goodwin, G., *The Janissaries*, London 2006.
Hannerz, U., *Cultural Complexity: Studies in the Social Organization of Meaning*, New York 1992.
Hannerz, U., "Diversity is Our Business", *American Anthropologist*, 112 (2010), 539–551.
Hobsbawm, E., *Nations and Nationalism since 1780*, 2nd ed, Cambridge 2012.
Huntington, S., *The Clash of Civilization and the Remaking of World Order*, New York, 1998.
Ikenberry, G. J., *After Victory*. Princeton NJ 2001.
Jackson, R., *The Global Covenant*, Oxford 2000.
Jacques, M., *When China Rules the World: Then End of the Western World and the Birth of a New Global Order*, 2nd ed., Harmondsworth 2012.
Jepperson, R. L./Wendt, A./Katzenstein, P. J., "Norms, Identity, and Culture in National Security", in Katzenstein, P. J. (ed.), *The Culture of National Security*, New York 1996, 33–75.
Kissinger, H., *World Order: Reflections on the Character of Nations and the Course of History*, London 2014.
Koskenniemi, M., *From Apology to Utopia: The Structure of Legal Argument*, 2nd ed., Cambridge 2005.
Krasner, S. D., *Sovereignty: Organized Hypocrisy*, Princeton NJ 1999.
Malik, K., "The Failure of Multiculturalism", *Foreign Affairs*, 94 (March/April 2015).
McCall, G. T./Simmons, J. L., *Identities and Interactions*, New York 1966.
Ning, C., *Lifanyuan and the Management of Population Diversity in Early Qing: 1653–1795*, Max Planck Institute for Social Anthropology, Working Paper 139, 2012.
O'Neill, B., *Honor, Symbols, and War*, Ann Arbor 2001.
Obama, B., President Barack Obama, United Nations Security Council, 24 September 2014.
Patten, A., *Equal Recognition: The Moral Foundations of Minority Rights*. Princeton NJ 2014.
Putnam, R. D., "E Pluribus Unum: Diversity and Community in the Twenty First Century", *Scandinavian Political Studies*, 30 (2007), 137–174.
Rae, H., *State Identities and the Homogenisation of Peoples*, Cambridge 2002.
Raymond. W, *Keywords*, London 2014.
Reus-Smit, C., *The Moral Purpose of the State*. Princeton NJ 1999.
Reus-Smit, C., "The Liberal International Order Reconsidered", in Friedman, R./Oskanian, K./Pachero-Pardo, R. (eds.), *After Liberalism*, London 2013, 167–186.

Rudd, K., "The West Isn't Ready for the Rise of China", *New Statesman* (2012), http://www.newstatesman.com/politics/international-politics/2012/07/kevin-rudd-west-isnt-ready-rise-china.

Ruggie, J. G., Continuity and Transformation in the World Polity: Toward a Neorealist Synthesis, *World Politics*, 83 (1983), 261–285.

Sewell, W., *Logics of History: Social Theory and Social Transformation*, Chicago 2005.

Shiyuan, H., "Ethnicities and Ethnic Relations", in Peilin, L. (ed.), *Chinese Society: Change and Transformation*, London 2012, 86–107.

Sturgis, P./Brunton-Smith, I./Kuha, J./Jackson, J., "Ethnic Diversity, Segregation, and Social Cohesion of Neighbourhoods in London", *Ethnic and Racial Studies*, 36 (2013), 1286–1309.

Swidler, A., "Culture in Action: Symbols and Strategies", *American Sociological Review*, 51 (1986), 273–286.

Swidler, A., *Talk of Love: How Culture Matters*, Chicago 2001.

Tully, J., *Strange Multiplicity: Constitutionalism in an Age of Diversity*, Cambridge 1995.

Wendt, A., Collective Identity Formation and the International State, *American Political Science Association*, 88 (1994), 384–396.

Wight, M., *Systems of States*, Leicester 1977.

Williams, R., *Keywords: A Vocabulary of Culture and Society*, London 2014.

Order in a Borderless World: Nomads Confront Globalization

Erik Ringmar

All problems of international politics are caused by borders.[1] It is at the border between us that things change; mine becomes yours and yours mine; flags are lowered and hoisted, passports requested, identities verified. It is the border that constitutes political entities as separate from each other and as sovereign. Borders make each state into a box and international relations into relations between boxes. It is control over the sovereign power created by the border which is at stake in civil wars. It is the border that protects the political leaders who commit crimes against their own populations. It is when the troops of a country are crossing the borders of its enemy that war no longer is a possibility but a fact.

So let us abolish borders. If there are no borders, there is no yours and no mine and nothing for political leaders, or minority groups, to fight over and no borders that can protect ruthless dictators. Without borders there can be no sovereignty and no wars. Fanciful and unrealistic though this suggestion sounds, it has actually been tried—well, sort of. In the last decades of the nineteenth-century, exchange expanded at an unprecedented rate, creating a networked world in which money, goods and people moved around without respect for national borders. During this, so called, 'first era of globalization', international shipping and railroad networks expanded dramatically; telegraph and telephone lines connected people; tariffs were lowered and banks linked up in an international financial system. To liberals, this suggested the possibility that peace on earth finally could be achieved. If everyone was sufficiently dependent on everyone else, the argument went, no one can afford to start a war. And the nineteenth-century was indeed exceptionally peaceful, at least in Europe.

---

1 I am grateful to Gunther Hellman, Iver Neumann, Brendan O'Leary and James C. Scott for suggestions and help with bibliographical references, and to audiences at the Goethe University, Frankfurt, and the CEU in Budapest, for comments.

This experiment came to an abrupt end when the First World War broke out in 1914. Borderlessness had not only brought an unprecedented level of economic prosperity but also made people's lives far more insecure than previously. They wanted their borders back; they wanted a proper home for themselves, and homes as always require solid walls and doors that can be securely bolted. The result was the welfare state, in its Bismarckian, Fabian and Social Democratic versions, but also the national state as defined by Nazis in Germany, Fascists in Italy and by Stalin in the Soviet Union. In the wake of the First World War, borders were reestablished all over Europe, and outside of Europe borders were reaffirmed as new states in the wake of the Second World War made themselves independent of their colonial masters. The twentieth-century was the century of borders. It was also more than anything the century of wars, civil wars and genocide.

For the past couple of decades, we seem to be repeating the nineteenth-century experiment. Money, goods and people are once again moving around with little concern for borders. In our 'second era of globalization', economic exchange has once again taken off and prosperity is spreading far more widely than ever previously. Once again the hopes of liberals have been awakened. We are once again all dependent on each other; just as in the nineteenth-century, no one can today afford to start a war. But with increasing exposure to world markets comes an increasing sense of vulnerability and thereby renewed fears. Borderlessness leads to homelessness and anxiety. Once again there are voices calling for protection—protection against the vagaries of markets, against the decline in sovereignty, against the influx of foreign migrants and refugees. Political leaders spouting nationalistic slogans are gaining in the polls. They promise to build us new homes, with solid walls and doors that can be securely bolted. The prospects are terrifying.

We want exchange and we want prosperity, but we also want protection. We want peace but also a home we can call our own. The question is whether, and how, the two can be combined. The question is how order can be established and maintained in a borderless world. The people best placed to answer such questions, we will suggest in this chapter, are nomads. Nomads are people who move around in order to make a living—hunters and gatherers who look for animals to hunt and plants to gather; pastoralists who follow their herds in search of new pastures; but also traders, sailors, truckers, circus people and tramps who follow the roads looking for opportunities and ways to survive. They all live in a world without borders, and this is where they have made a home for themselves. They are exposed to be sure, but they have devised strategies to reduce their vulnerability. If we today increasingly are living the lives of nomads, and if our lives in the future will become more nomadic still, it would seem we have a lot to learn from people who always have lived in a borderless world.[2]

The Anti-nomadic Prejudice of the European State

Anti-nomadic sentiments may be the most widely shared of all prejudices, uniting sedentary peoples around the globe regardless of their color, creed or sexuality. To this day, despite our proud boasts of acknowledging "differences", many do not even recognize their anti-nomadic prejudices for what they are. The life of a nomad is so obviously wrong. Consider the European state. When political philosophers in the early modern era discussed what it was that made the state legitimate, their answer was that the state was legitimate since it had rescued us from a peripatetic existence. And when the state subsequently proceeded to assert its power over society, repressive measures were put in place against vagrants, tramps and travelers—against all people, that is, without a fixed address. Likewise, when the European state, from the sixteenth-century onward, went on colonial exploits in non-European parts of the world, it occupied the land of the natives on the pretext that the nomads who lived there had failed to make productive use of it.

Political Philosophy

That politics requires borders is obvious already from the word itself.[3] 'Politics' is derived from *polis*, the political community created by the Greek city-state. More than anything, the Greeks distinguished the *polis* from nature. The city was a human creation which took human beings out of nature and thereby allowed them to develop their full potential. Man is a

---

[2] An argument to be further developed in Ringmar, *Political Theory for Nomads*.
[3] See further Ringmar, The Anti-Nomadic Bias of Political Theory.

zoon politikon, wrote Aristotle; an animal who needs the state. To be a citizen was to be a civilized person, and to be banished from the city was thus the harshest of all punishment. Nature is where you go wild, go crazy, like the women in Euripides' *The Bacchæ* who left their hearths and their looms in pursuit of their god. But nature was fascinating too and those who dared to venture beyond the city-gates could visit places like Arcadia, a province in the heart of the Peloponnese.[4] It was in Arcadia that the nomads tended their sheep. The nomads lived in a pre-political, that is, in a pre-human, condition, but there was at the same time an innocence to their lives which easily lent itself to pastoral *rêveries*.

In early modern Europe, the problem confronted by all political philosophers was how to give legitimacy to the state. With what right, they asked, could the state coerce the people subject to it, make them pay taxes and die in its wars? In reply the philosophers imagined a 'state of nature', a condition in which human beings were imagined to have lived prior the establishment of the first state. If this original condition only could be shown to have been sufficiently repellent, the state could be presented as a necessary improvement and thereby as legitimate. The state of nature was usually envisioned as a large forest in which people roamed around without a fixed abode. The state of nature, that is, was a state of nomadism. Thomas Hobbes' version of the argument is perhaps the most famous. Mustering all his rhetorical powers, Hobbes described a pre-state world in which man's life had been "solitary, poor, nasty, brutish, and short."[5] And although John Locke's state of nature was a rather more benign condition, a person's labor was never secure since there was no way of protecting one's property.[6] The solution suggested by both Hobbes and Locke was that people should subject themselves to a political authority. The state was legitimate, said Hobbes, since it kept people 'in awe'; the state was legitimate, said Locke, since it protected the fences which industrious citizens put up.

Although the state of nature was a rhetorical device, it was often taken as a historical reality. In an account popular among political philosophers in the eighteenth-century, human history was divided into four separate

---

4 Hartog, *Memories of Odysseus*, 133–50.
5 Hobbes, *Leviathan*, 78; See also Mill, Civilization, 161–162.
6 Locke, *Two Treatises of Government*, 208–30.

stages.[7] The first stage was a society made up of hunters and gatherers, the second stage a society of pastoralists—after which followed agricultural and then commercial society. Each stage represented an improvement over its predecessor and nomadic societies were for that reason the representatives of an earlier stage of human history. To visit a nomadic society was to travel back in time.

The existence of the state is still occasionally defended by references to an imaginary nomadic condition. There are roving bandits, the political economist Mancur Olson explained, and there are stationary bandits.[8] While roving bandits have an incentive to take and destroy, stationary bandits develop a stake in the economic success of their victims. Before long the stationary bandits begin to protect people from their roving colleagues, asking for taxes in return. The result is a state, and it was the state as it came to develop over the course of the centuries that eventually made all other political institutions possible. It is since we no longer are nomads that we can form a society, live in security and freedom, and together determine our fate.

State-building

The anti-nomadic prejudice is obvious also from the practices in which the state engaged. In early modern Europe, where popular uprisings were a constant threat, it was imperative for the state to control people, and people who stayed in one place were a lot easier to control. In addition, sedentary people were easier to tax, to call up for military service, and to subject to various reforms. As a result, repressive policies were put in place against anyone who lived an 'unsettled life': most obviously the Roma, the Yenish, the Sami of northern Scandinavia, but also Irish travelers, tinkers, hobos, circus people, 'wandering Jews', and many others. This history of prejudice and repression is, embarrassingly, ongoing.[9]

The problem, sedentary people have always insisted, is that nomadic people cannot be trusted. There is a systematic lack of trust between

---

7 See, inter alia, Ferguson, *History of Civil Society*, 543–68; Smith, *An Inquiry into the Nature and Causes of the Wealth of Nations*.
8 Olson, *Power And Prosperity*; Cf. Tilly, War Making and State Making as Organized Crime, 169–91.
9 MacKay et al., Before and after Borders.

people who are on the move and those who stay put. Trust after all requires repeated interaction before it can be established; people need to see each other again and again—without a notion of when their last encounter will take place—before they can come to properly assess one another.[10] People living unsettled lives have no commitment to a particular locality, to local people and their ways of life. While all societies may have strong norms against cheating fellow members of their own community, they generally care far less about non-members. The problem for nomads is that while sedentary people mainly interact with people who are familiar to them, they interact mainly with strangers.

Consider the rudimentary welfare policies put in place in the early modern era. Poor relief was given by each parish and, according to what in Germany was known as the *Heimat* principle, only to parishioners.[11] Since they imposed a cost on the community, the number of people eligible for support was kept as low as possible and outsiders were consequently chased away. Those who refused to leave could be whipped, put in stock, branded or imprisoned, and members of the Roma community could, in parts of Europe, be hunted and killed at will.[12] The prejudice against vagrants continued even as the developing market economy increasingly came to produce them. From the end of the eighteenth-century, fewer hands were needed in the countryside, and those who could not find work in a factory—or those whom the vagaries of the market made redundant—often took to the road. The police—established as a regular force all over Europe in the first part of the nineteenth-century—had repression of vagrancy as one of its principal tasks.[13] In the nineteenth-century vagrants were often transported to the colonies.

In implementing these policies, the state felt history to be on its side. After all, nomadism represented an earlier stage of human society, and the more the division of labor expanded, the more marginal nomadism was bound to become.[14] In an efficient economy, plants are grown, not gathered; animals are reared, not hunted; and people work productively in factories. These obvious facts have been taught by development agencies and international aid organizations to this day. Before the economy can

---

10 Cf. Wintrobe, Some Economics of Ethnical Capital Formation and Conflict, 43–70.
11 Lucassen, Eternal Vagrants?, 71.
12 Ibid., 61.
13 Ibid., 67.
14 Kradin, Nomadism, Evolution and World-Systems, 368–88.

take off and acquire a measure of self-sustained growth, the steppes have to be fenced in and the deserts irrigated. Nomads should be resettled in towns. By liberal reformers, acting with the best of intentions, such policies have been justified in terms of 'inclusion' and 'integration'. If we are to put a stop to the prejudices against them, we must convince the travelers to stop traveling. In modern society everyone must live somewhere, at a fixed address. The nomads must register to vote and register for all the services provided by the state; their children must go to school and to the doctor. Only people who can be located can be cared for and controlled.[15]

Colonialism

Compare the international practices in which European states engaged. From around the year 1500, Europeans came to invade and occupy first the Americas, then Asia and Africa, and at the end of the nineteenth-century only a few non-colonized parts of the world remained. The question was with what right people outside of Europe were deprived of their land. In his *De Indis de Jure Belli*, 1532, Francisco de Vitoria argued that God had given human beings the earth in order to cultivate it and that land which lays fallow legitimately can be appropriated.[16] And yet, rather courageously, de Vitoria sided with the natives. Since it was clear that they did use the land, he concluded, the conquistadors had no right to simply take it. In the end these legal arguments were ignored of course and the natives lost their land anyway, yet de Vitoria's argument set the terms in which colonial appropriation would continue to be discussed.

The British were quick to use de Vitoria to their own advantage. Wherever they went in their travels, they discovered uninhabited lands, not cultivated by anyone, and whenever they did, they declared themselves ready, able and willing to carry out God's plan. Nowhere in the Americas or in Africa were there any fences, they argued; there was no property and hence no property rights. Since the end of the nineteenth-century the term *terra nullius* has been applied to these supposedly uninhabited lands.[17] A *terra*, 'land', is *nullius*, 'no one's', as long as it does not belong to anyone, as judged by European standards. The rituals by means of which these lands

---

15 MacKay et al., Before and after Borders.
16 Fitzmaurice, *The Genealogy of Terra Nullius*, 1–15.
17 Fitzmaurice, *The Genealogy of Terra Nullius*.

were appropriated varied from one European country to the next: the Spaniards would plant a flag and read a declaration; the Dutch and the Portuguese would make a map; but the British would start building fences.[18]

These legal arguments were the basis for a sharp distinction between people of three different kinds: civilized people, barbarians and savages.[19] The civilized people were Europeans of course, while 'barbarians' were people who lived in the despotic kingdoms in Asia—people who had a state but a state of a very different kind than the European. 'Savages', finally, were those who lived in a condition of statelessness. The prime examples of savages were hunters, gatherers and pastoralists. While Europeans had an obligation to help and protect them, they could also make war against them if the situation so required. In fact, since they by definition were outside of the community of civilized states, the Europeans could fight savages with savage methods if need be.[20] This is how the civilized Europeans came to commit genocides in places like Tasmania, Tierra del Fuego and Southwest Africa.

An Experiment in Borderlessness

Then began a social experiment of sorts. In the latter part of the nineteenth-century, life in the world created by sovereign states became far more nomadic than previously. The reason was above all that economic resources began moving around: goods and services were traded between countries at an unprecedented rate and capital was flowing to the places were it provided the highest yields. With the change in economic opportunities, people began moving too. Yet many also felt far more insecure than previously. People felt rootless and homeless. Picking up on such sentiments, an anti-nomadic, anti-globalization, rhetoric gained ground. All humans need a home, went the argument, and all nations need to protect their borders.

---

18 Seed, *Ceremonies of Possession*, 16–40.
19 See, for example, Lorimer, *Institutes*, 2:101.
20 Ringmar, How to Fight Savage Tribes, 264–83; See further Lemarchand, *Forgotten Genocides*.

The First Era of Globalization

In order to understand the process of globalization as it took place in the course of the nineteenth-century we have to keep two quite different pictures in mind at the same time. The first picture shows us the apotheosis of the state. It was only in the nineteenth-century that the process of state formation came to be completed and only now that the state could live up to its long-standing claims to sovereignty. For one thing, its borders were for the first time clearly defined.[21] In the course of the nineteenth-century states expanded to fill up all available space; there were no longer any moving frontiers and no fussy hinterlands beyond them. Everywhere—although most famously perhaps on the Great Plains of North America—this expansion took place at the expense of nomadic peoples. In Africa the last white spaces on the European maps were filled in, and at the Berlin Conference in 1885 the entire continent was given borders, and divided up, between the colonial powers. In Europe itself the patchwork map made up of assorted political entities was radically simplified—above all as a result of the unification of Italy, 1861, and Germany, 1872. The entire world was now exhaustively divided between states, and each state was vastly more powerful than previously. The state was in control of its territory and its people; taxes could be levied and policies could be implemented by a powerful bureaucracy.

The second picture shows us a world which is far more tightly connected than ever previously. The states were networked, as it were, and in the networks things began moving around at an ever quickening pace. Various technical inventions played a crucial role in this regard.[22] International shipping expanded as a result of stream-driven ships with iron hulls that greatly reduced transportation costs. Railroad expansion created national networks which in turn were connected to the international railroad network. By means of the railroad it was possible to sell far more things to far more people, and as a result far larger companies could be created. Since railroads required standardized timetables, a unified system for measuring time—a world time—was for the first time established. Meanwhile, inventions such as the telegraph, and later the telephone, made it possible to communicate with far away places in real

---

21 Osterhammel, *The Transformation of the World*, 322–91.
22 Ibid., 710–43; On the contermporary use of the network metaphor, see Otis, *Networking*, 49–80.

time.[23] Suddenly, from the 1880s onward, every place on earth was related to every other. The world was one, not many.

In these networks goods, services and money were sent around, but also people and ideas. Factory owners needed natural resources to feed to their machines, and in the latter part of the nineteenth-century there was an explosive demand for tin, rubber and cotton in particular.[24] But the factory owners needed customers for their products too and international trade boomed, in particular after mid-century when tariffs were reduced or abolished. An international network of banks created an international financial system and it was suddenly easy for a person in London to invest in South African mines or in Latin American railroad shares. Thanks to the international gold standard prices were easily compared. And as we would expect, people began moving around too. In the course of the nineteenth-century, some 85 percent of Europeans moved—70 percent within their respective countries, the rest abroad.[25] Between 1815 and 1914 at least 82 million people moved across borders—three times more people than in the twentieth-century.[26] As a result the ethnic composition of the United States was radically altered, adding far more Italians, Poles and Jews to the mix, and in Argentina, in 1914, 58 percent of the population had either been born abroad or were children of first-generation immigrants.[27] During no other time in human history had this many people been on the move.

In the course of the nineteenth-century, in other words, borders were first affirmed and strengthened and then superseded. Yet this is not to say that states became redundant. On the contrary, states were more than anything the units which constituted the networked world and they were as such the first ones to benefit from it. The most obvious gains were economic. What we can obtain from others there is no need to make ourselves, and by specializing on what we are best at making, we become more competitive. As a result of specialization, the world economy became more productive, living standards rose across the board, and each state expanded its reach and its commitments correspondingly. But there were political

---

23 See further Kern, *The Culture of Time and Space 1880-1918*.
24 Pollard, Free Trade, Protectionism, and the World Economy; Osterhammel, *The Transformation of the World*, 728–29.
25 Schulze, *States, Nations and Nationalism*, 141.
26 Osterhammel, *The Transformation of the World*, 154.
27 Ibid., 156.

benefits too. As the British journalist Norman Angell explained, in a world in which everyone depends on everyone else, no one can afford to start a war.[28] Peace on earth suddenly appeared to be a realistic prospect. "As we have outgrown the duel," as Andrew Carnegie put it, "so have we outgrown homicidal war."[29]

Culture vs. Civilization

We find the same two pictures if we make a distinction between culture, on the one hand, and civilization, on the other. The nineteenth-century was a time when culture for the first time became national in scope.[30] As a part of their program of self-assertion all European states created national symbols for themselves—flags, national anthems—as well as national institutions—academies, opera houses, theaters, museums and so on. In the newly established public school systems, a national history was taught together with standardized, national, ways of speaking, writing and thinking. As a result, the immense cultural variety that previously had existed was marginalized or entirely wiped out.[31] And yet, at the same time, and as a consequently of participating in increasingly tightly integrated networks, states also became more and more alike. They were all being "civilized".[32]

Consider the metaphors implied by this terminology. Culture refers to 'cultivation', that is, to the 'tilling of the land'. To cultivate a plant is to care for it and to make it grow. Metaphorically speaking, what is being cultivated by a culture is the human soul—compare individuals and societies that 'flourish', 'flower' or 'bloom'. Thus understood, culture is reserved for sedentary people. In order to grow things, after all, we need to stay sufficiently long in one place to plant the crop, water and weed it, to harvest and store it. In order to protect what we grow, we drive stakes into the ground and build fences which separates what is ours from that which belongs to others. Engaged in these activities, sedentary people develop a

---

28 See the Synopsis, in Angell, *Great Illusion*, vii–xiii; For a critical assessment, see Carr, *The Twenty Years' Crisis*.
29 Carnegie, The Baseless Fear of War, 80.
30 See, *inter alia*, Hobsbawm, *Nations and Nationalism since 1780*, 80–100; Schulze, *States, Nations and Nationalism*, 114–36.
31 Weber, *Peasants into Frenchmen*, 67–114; The analogous case of Thailand is discussed in Winichakul, *Siam Mapped*, 81–94.
32 Gong, *Standard of Civilization*; Ringmar, *Liberal Barbarism*, 90–93.

strong attachment to a particular location. They make a place out of space.[33] These few acres are the land that feeds us, which fed our ancestors and which will feed our descendants in turn.

To nomads this makes no sense. Nomads do not grow anything. They never stay long enough in one place to cultivate the land and they never commit themselves to a particular location by driving stakes into the ground. We would consequently expect nomads to be low on culture. And this is indeed the case. Or rather, all of their cultural artifacts have to be movable. They produce songs and folktales and clothes and talismans but make neither monuments nor pictures to hang on walls. Moreover, in the history of warfare between nomadic and sedentary societies, nomads have often pulled up stakes and destroyed crops. Fences are an encumbrance since they block movement and planted crops are an abomination to the extent that they replace the grassland on which animals can feed. In this way nomads not only deprive sedentary peoples of the bases of their power but they also assure the freedom of movement on which their own power depends. More generally, nomadic warriors are notorious for their disrespect for cultural artifacts. They have often indiscriminately destroyed cultural treasures, burnt down libraries and entire cities—the Mongol destruction of Baghdad in 1258 is only the most notorious example.

Yet this is also how nomads become the agents of civilization. If culture takes its metaphorical basis in agriculture, civilization takes its metaphorical basis in exchange. Everything that allows exchange to flourish helps spread civilization.[34] Civilization depends on the unencumbered circulation of goods, people, ideas, faiths and ways of life. Exchange means that things can be compared and judged in relation to each other; exchange provides you with a choice; you can choose the better or the cheaper option. Civilization is for that reason constitutionally opposed to walls. Walls block your vision and make it impossible for outsiders to see what you are doing; walls protect the corrupt and incompetent, high prices and low qualities. Compare the way the way the Mongols destroyed the walls of every city they conquered and the way they extended and cared for the network of routes—the 'Silk Road'—which helped disseminate Chinese inventions like the printing press, the compass and gunpowder. Or compare the way the Arabs, originally a band of

---

33 Tuan, *Space and Place*, 67–84; Ingold, *Perception of the Environment*, 153–287.
34 Ringmar, *Liberal Barbarism*, 90–93.

Bedouins from the Arabian peninsula, acted as intermediaries between Asia, Europe and Africa, helping to civilize the Europeans.[35]

Or compare the way the networked world created in the nineteenth-century came to spread civilization by destroying culture. It is the 'profit motive', Karl Marx and Friedrich Engels famously argued in *The Communist Manifesto*, 1848, which has set the Europeans chasing around the world. And once the search for profits came to replace all other concerns, societies were everywhere dramatically transformed; the profit motive destroyed feudal relations and replaced them with market relations. "The cheap prices of its commodities are the heavy artillery with which it batters down all Chinese walls." "It compels all nations, on the pain of extinction, to adopt the bourgeois mode of production; it compels them to introduce what it calls civilization into their midst, *i.e.*, to become bourgeois themselves. In a word, it creates a world after its own image."[36]

As a result of this destruction which has continued to this day, living standards have increased, standards of education and health have improved, notions of democracy and freedom of expression have spread more widely. At the end of this process, we will all be civilized but there will be no culture left.

The new Homelessness

If you are a sedentary person, deeply rooted in the soil, a nomadic lifestyle will always appear as a form of homelessness. This was also the conclusion reached by many contemporary observers around the turn of the twentieth-century. Modern society, they concluded, had made people homeless. "We have left the land and have embarked," as Friedrich Nietzsche put it in 1882. "We have burned our bridges behind us—indeed, we have gone further and have destroyed the land behind us—Woe, when you feel homesick for the land as if it had offered more freedom—and there is no longer any 'land'."[37]

Nietzsche was born in Prussia but renounced his German citizenship when he became professor at the university of Basel, in Switzerland, in

---

[35] Weatherford, *Genghis Khan and the Making of the Modern World*, 19; Ringmar, The Great Wall of China Does Not Exist.
[36] Marx and Engels, *Manifesto of the Communist Party*, 18.
[37] Nietzsche, *The Gay Science*, sec. 124.

1869. After that he was stateless. And once he, a decade later, left his position at the university, he was more or less homeless too, spending the summers in Switzerland and the winters living in boarding-houses and cheap hotels all over Italy.[38] Nietzsche called himself "a good European", which he equated with homeless, stateless, and nomadism.[39]

There were many homeless writers like Nietzsche around the turn of the twentieth-century. Another example is Rudyard Kipling, the author of *The Jungle Book*, 1894, and many other much-read, and loved, stories. Born in Bombay in 1865, Kipling was educated in England, but returned to India, only to go off to live in the United States, South Africa, India again and then England again. Writing about Kipling's life, the English journalist G.K. Chesterton called him "a philanderer of the nations."[40] In no place had Kipling lived the life of a local, Chesterton pointed out; he was neither an Indian, an Englishman, an American nor anything else. Kipling has loved many countries the way a man may have been the lover of many women without ever having loved a single one of them. It is only the properly rooted person, Chesterton pointed out, the person with a home, who can understand the roots, and homes, of others. Kipling "is a man of the world, with all the narrowness that belongs to those imprisoned in that planet."

"He knows England as an intelligent English gentleman knows Venice. He has been to England a great many times; he has stopped there for long visits. But he does not belong to it, or to any place; and the proof of it is this, that he thinks of England as a place. The moment we are rooted in a place, the place vanishes. We live like a tree with the whole strength of the universe."[41]

Chesterton himself, who today mainly is remembered as the author of the *Father Brown* series of detective stories, was a Catholic and a conservative, and Kipling, to him, symbolized everything he found most abhorrent about modern society. Kipling was a cosmopolitan and an imperialist. In the course of his peripatetic travels he had made himself homeless, and the superficiality of his cosmopolitanism and the cruelty of his imperialism were the inevitable consequences of his peripatetic state. "The globe-

---

38 A detailed itinerary is provided in Krell and Bates, *The Good European*.
39 Nietzsche, *The Gay Science*, sec. 377.
40 Chesterton, On Mr. Rudyard Kipling and Making the World Small, 48; On Kipling's life, see further Gilmour, *Long Recessional*.
41 Chesterton, On Mr. Rudyard Kipling and Making the World Small, 49.

trotter," said Chesterton, "lives in a smaller world than the peasant."[42] "The man in the saloon steamer has seen all the races of men, and his is thinking of the things that divide men [...] The man in the cabbage field has seen nothing at all; but he is thinking of the things that unite men— hunger and babies, and the beauty of women, and the promise or menace of the sky."[43]

It is easy to take Chesterton's side in this argument. He is the wittier of the two writers and he makes Kipling into a rather ridiculous character. Moreover, Chesterton's position has an intuitive appeal. By prioritizing the local and the everyday over the universal and exceptional, and by celebrating simple pleasures, he is insisting that there is a way to make a life for ourselves also in modern society. He is trying to help us find a way back home.

Chesterton was not alone in writing in this vein. 'Homelessness' is a good label for the existential malaise which plagued many people in modern society, and the obvious solution was to help them create new homes for themselves. The rhetoric of home and homelessness came particularly easily to conservative writers. For example: in his ruminations on the notion of 'Being', the philosopher Martin Heidegger identified *Angst*, 'anxiety', as the fundamental mood of modern society.[44] Anxiety renders the world *unheimlich*, Heidegger argued, a term usually translated as 'uncanny', but which is better rendered as 'un-home-like'. As a result of our anxiety, we suffer from *Heimweh*, 'homesickness'.[45] However, as Heidegger came to conclude in the 1930s, if Germans only follow the lead of their *Führer* they can be reconnected to their community and its destiny.[46] A national *Heimat*, a 'homeland', was going to be created for all Germans, the Nazi propaganda promised; that is, a home for everybody who shared the same blood and the same soil.

---

42 Ibid.
43 Ibid., 50.
44 Heidegger, *Being and Time*, 228–35.
45 Cf. for example Heidegger's address to his fellow townspeople in Heidegger, Meßkirch's Seventh Centennial, 41–57.
46 The literature on Heidegger and the Nazis is enormous. For an introduction see Harries, Heidegger as a Political Thinker, 642–69; Cf. Ringmar, Heidegger on Willpower and the Mood of Modernity.

But the rhetoric of home and homelessness existed in a left-wing version too.[47] In Sweden in the 1930s, the ruling Social Democrats promised to make the country into a *folkhem*, a 'home for the people', in which every Swede was going to find a place.[48] Just as in a regular family, the welfare state would care for its members while exercising strict control over their lives. Like all homes, the *folkhem* had a roof and walls which protected its members from the vicissitudes of the outside world, and it had a door which could be bolted and closed shut. As the Social Democrats made clear, however, this was a home for Swedes, and while Jews never were persecuted, nomadic groups such as the Roma and the Sami were. In Sweden, eugenics policies were in place well into the 1960s.[49]

Principles of Nomadic Society

For the past couple of decades—since the 1980s—we seem to be repeating the experiment with borderlessness conducted in the nineteenth-century. Money, goods and people are once again moving around in expanding and ever tighter networks. As a result, economic development has taken off and prosperity is spreading far more widely than ever before—countries in Africa are finally developing; China and India are 'taking off'. But with increasing exposure to world markets comes an increasing sense of vulnerability and thereby renewed fears. Borderlessness leads to homelessness and anxiety. Once again there are voices calling for protection, a halt to migration, and political leaders with xenophobic agendas are gaining in the polls. They promise to build us new homes, with solid walls and doors that can be securely bolted.

Human desires seem to be incompatible, in other words. We want exchange and the prosperity it brings but we also want the protection which a home affords. We want to live with others but also on our own; we want to be free but also rooted; we love the local but aspire to the universal. Yet, the reason why these ideals seem incompatible, we will argue, is only that

---

47 On the similarities in policies, see Garraty, The New Deal, National Socialism, and the Great Depression, 907–44.
48 Hentilä, The Origins of the Folkhem Ideology in Swedish Social Democracy, 323–45; Ringmar, *Surviving Capitalism*, 106–107.
49 Spektorowski and Mizrachi, Eugenics and the Welfare State in Sweden, 333–52.

sedentary people find it difficult to combine them. For nomads, however, this is easy; they bridge dichotomies such as these all the time. There is order to their societies although they live in a borderless world. Although the neo-nomads of the twenty-first-century would seem to have next to nothing in common with the pastoralists of yore, the logic of a peripatetic life will always be fundamentally different from a sedentary logic. Learning more about the logic of nomadic societies, we will be better prepared to meet the challenges of globalization. Indeed learning from nomadic societies might turn out to be an urgent task. Consider the following short list of lessons.[50]

Displacement

Sedentary people make space into place by dwelling in it, we said, but it can never work that way for nomads. They know places too but only as passed through, not as dwelt in. Consider their homes. Nomads live in tents or in other simple structures which they can collapse in a few hours and take with them to the next place they go. Putting the tent back up, they are immediately at home in the new location. The Mongols plant an *ürga*, a lasso on a pole, outside of their *ger*, tent, in order to show to outsiders that they are at home. The place where the *ürga* is planted is the center of their universe. In much the same fashion, the nomadic Achilpa of Australia use a pole made from the trunk of a gum tree to denote the axis which connects the earth and the sky. Carrying the pole with them they are always in their own world and they can always communicate with the sky.[51]

Not surprisingly, nomads never build cities. Genghis Khan himself had no capital but took instead his bureaucracy with him in a tent placed on a horse-drawn carriage. The places subsequently known as the 'capitals' of the Mongol empire, like Karakorum in Mongolia and Sarai in Russia, were in fact nothing more than large collections of tents. Since this is the case, there is never much left to see once the nomads have moved on. Nothing is today left of Karakorum or Sarai. In Ulaanbaatar, the capital of today's Mongolia, some 60 percent of the population still live in *ger*.[52]

---

50 See further Ringmar, *Political Theory for Nomads*; Cf. Neumann and Wigen, The Importance of the Eurasian Steppe, 319–23.
51 Eliade, *The Sacred and the Profane*, 33; Ingold, *Perception of the Environment*, 181–82.
52 Diener and Hagen, City of Felt and Concrete, 623.

We would expect this peripatetic existence to cease in death. Made of dust, we would expect nomads too to return to dust. Except that often they do not. After all, a grave would have to be protected and commemorated and as such it would be an encumbrance which would fix and constrain their movements. For that reason nomads in Tibet often exposed the bodies of their dead on mountain tops, to be picked apart by carrion birds.[53] Among nomadic groups in South East Asia too it has been common not to bury the dead but instead to put the corpses in trees. Through these so called 'sky burials' the bodies take flight. In fact, not even Genghis Khan had his own grave, and it is only after the end of Communism, with the rise of Mongolian nationalism, that monuments commemorating him have been erected. Gods may be displaced in the same fashion. Although nomads certainly may worship deities that are located in a particular place, such as a tree which they regularly visit on their journeys, it is more convenient to place the god on top of a high mountain which can be seen from far away across the steppe. Or, as the Mongols did, to worship Tengri, the god of the blue sky.[54] The sky, after all, is always with you.

The Band

When Chesterton defended the local over the universal what he had in mind was more than anything his own local neighborhood. He liked the idea of neighbors who can get together over a meal, a beer and a conversation. Yet nomads have no neighbors; no one lives next door since there are no next doors. Instead social ties are forged with the people who travel together, at the same time and in the same direction. This is the band, the group, the gang, the posse. The band includes family members and members of one's clan, but often also extraneous people who have joined up along the way. Yet the band often forms imaginary bonds with other people, and other bands, who make a life for themselves in the same fashion—there is a brotherhood of hobos and a fellowship of truckers, sailors, circus people and tinkers.

---

53 Martin, On the Cultural Ecology of Sky Burial on the Himalayan Plateau, 353–70.
54 Bira, Mongolian Tenggerism and Modern Globalism, 107–17; Cf. Berman, *Wandering God*.

Relations within the band are largely egalitarian, and more egalitarian certainly than relations among sedentary peoples.[55] Since nomads have no fixed property, they cannot assemble the kinds of wealth through which sedentary people like to distinguish themselves from each other. Instead wealth is measured in terms of the number of animals a person owns, and although herds can vary considerably in size too, the conditions of life on the road make it difficult to translate this wealth into social distinctions. Moreover, nomadic societies have a low degree of division of labor. There are specialized tasks like putting up tents, hunting and foraging—and navigators and path-finders will obviously occupy a privileged position—yet in the end every member of the group is engaged in much the same project.

Trust, we said, is established as people repeatedly come to interact with one another without any notion of when their last interaction will take place. Since members of the nomadic group interact very closely, the level of trust between them is high. Moreover, the singular quality of their way of life—and the prejudice directed against them—mean that they often have a strong sense of an imagined community which encompasses all fellow travelers. Compare, for example, the elaborate dictionary of signs which hobos in the United States have developed in order to share information. A horizontal zigzag on a gate signifies 'a barking dog'; a picture of a cat 'a kind lady lives here.'[56] Conversely, we would expect there to be little trust between nomads and the people they encounter on their journeys.

Paths

But nomads are not moving around at random. There is a pattern to their movements; they follow a certain path. Which paths that are chosen depends on the geographical distribution of opportunities. Thus pastoralists often move their herds from summer pastures in the mountains to winter pastures in the valleys, and hunters and gatherers move in relation to the seasonal variation in the availability of game and plants.[57] Other nomads

---

55 The degree of equality has been debated. Two more skeptical accounts are Asad, Equality in Nomadic Social Systems?, 57–65; Sneath, *The Headless State*.
56 Moon, *Done and Been*, 24.
57 Nugent and Sanchez, Tribes, Chiefs, and Transhumance, 87–113.

move depending on the availability of jobs. You follow the circus as it goes on tour in the summer; move eastward in October to help out with the *vendange*; moor your canoe when the rivers freeze over in the winter.[58]

Together the paths create a network which allows us to move not only from one place to another but from one place to everywhere else in the network of paths. Compare the kinds of maps that nomads use. Nomads care little for territory understood as measurable, and depictable, units of land. Territory that stretches endlessly in all directions has no proper measure and is for that reason not depictable. Moreover, territory in the far distance is always perceived by the human mind as two- and not as three-dimensional.[59] For this reason, the maps of nomadic societies are not maps of places but maps of how to get to places. A place exists not in space but as a node in a matrix of movement and maps show not territories but networks of places linked by paths.[60] Sedentary people often laugh at maps like these and say they are incorrect, but they are not poor descriptions of territory but instead perfect descriptions of how to reach a certain destination. Consider the London tube map which provides just the information you need to get from Mornington Crescent to Turnpike Lane.

Nodes

In all networks there are nodes. Although nomads are impossible to coerce, they will quite happily assemble at the same places at regular intervals. Nodes are intersections where roads come together; hubs where we change planes and board ferries; markets where we sell products and buy supplies; places where rivers are more easily forded and mountains crossed. Above all nodes are hostels, inns and caravanserais where we can get a good night's rest and a hot meal.

Nodes such as these are where nomads are most likely to make friends with people outside of their own group. By talking, eating and drinking with strangers they share information and gossip. It is also at the nodes that a measure of control most effectively can be imposed on them. It is when people show up to trade that they may agree to pay a tax. This gives

---

58 For an abundance of examples see, inter alia, Davies, *The Autobiography of a Super-Tramp*; Podruchny, *Making the Voyageur World*.
59 Bollnow, *Human Space*, 47.
60 Ingold, *Perception of the Environment*, 219, 228.

political authorities a measure of power and makes it possible to subject the nomads to assorted welfare programs. It is at markets that the children of nomads get medical examinations and where international aid agencies vaccinate them against epidemics.

Conflicts

Relations among nomadic groups are often conflictual but the conflicts are best described as raids not as wars. After all, there is no land to fight over—no land which can be invaded and occupied—and there is no point in appropriating things which the raiders cannot take with them. Instead conflicts concern access to productive resources—grazing rights above all and control over animals, women and labor. The only time when these conflicts temporarily cease is when the groups turn their energies away from each other and towards an external enemy. This is how the Bedouins of the Arabian peninsula came to conquer the Middle East and North Africa after the death of Muhammad in 632 C.E. This is also how the Mongols came to conquer most of the Eurasian land mass once their leader, Temüjin, was made into "Genghis Khan" in 1206. The leaders of such expansions are faithfully followed as long as they are successful and able to deliver booty to their followers.

When it comes to warfare, nomads have several advantages over sedentary populations.[61] They are highly mobile, first of all, and can move far more quickly on their horses or camels than peasant armies can march on foot. As a result armies made up of farmers will easily find themselves outflanked and surrounded. In addition, nomads are good hunters—a skill which quite easily can be adapted for military use. The coordination required to catch a herd of wild deer is not that different from the coordination required to successfully attack an enemy, and someone who can shoot arrows from the back of a galloping horse can kill human beings too. Because of their speed, nomads can often cover large tracts of land and are only stopped by cities that are sufficiently fortified. Yet both Arabs and Mongols quickly learned the secrets of siege warfare.

Since armies made up of nomads never have to defend a particular place they are more likely to engage in skirmishes than in head-on battles.

---

61 A classical account is Gibbon, *The History of the Decline and Fall of the Roman Empire*, vol. 3, chap. 26.

To them there is no essential military difference between an advance and a retreat. Since they prefer to flee rather than to stand their ground and fight to the death, nomads have often been called 'cowards' by sedentary populations. But by fleeing they can easily regroup and live to fight another day. As a military tactic, the Mongols would often set traps for their enemies. After having besieged a town, they would retreat, inviting the defenders to pursue them. Then the pursuers would be ambushed and picked off one by one.

Decision-making

The lack of borders means that politics, and the people who are the subjects of politics, cannot be contained. Those who cannot be contained cannot be coerced. If the state is making trouble for you, you can just run away—into the jungle, the steppe or across the arctic wasteland. The agents of the state may try to follow you of course but with a decent headstart and a good pair of horses the odds are in your favor. Under such conditions the fences which constituted the material preconditions for Lockean theorizing cannot be defended, and Hobbes' Leviathan will inspire no awe if it cannot capture those who offend against it. Political life cannot be based on a contract.

For this reason, politics does not take place in any one place. Nomads have no presidential palaces, parliament buildings or government offices. Politics, as a result, can never be understood in theatrical terms. There is no pomp and circumstance intended to impress large audiences. Instead politics happens in person-to-person relationships and through everyday practices. Nomadic society forms a network, not a hierarchy, and as a network it can be influenced only sequentially, one node at a time. Expulsion from the group is by far the most powerful way to punish transgressors. In a sufficiently harsh climate, the prospect of making it on one's own is sufficiently daunting to provide an effective deterrent.

Nomadic societies are not democracies but instead decisions are typically made by the leaders of each household; that is, most commonly, the oldest males.[62] Yet since members of the group always can threaten to defect to another group or start a group of their own, ordinary members

---

62 Lewis, *A Pastoral Democracy*.

have a considerable amount of power. Suggestions cannot be ignored but have to be listened to. The result is a consensual forms of decision-making based on established customs. Periodically the leaders of the respective bands will get together to make decisions for society as a whole, broker peace between feuding factions or settle issues of grazing rights and inheritance. The *kurultai* of the Mongols was such a gathering of elders and in conflict-ridden Somalia consensual methods of conflict resolution have recently proven more effective than arbitration by international organizations.

International Politics Between Earth and Sky

All human beings make a life for themselves between the earth and the sky.[63] The earth is where we dwell; it is the earth which feeds us; the earth in which we one day will rest, forever concealed and protected. But as long as we are alive we are also open to the sky. The sky is infinite and boundless. There are no places in the sky where we can make a home for ourselves, instead everything we find there is on the move. It is to the sky that smoke rises, together with our dreams and prayers, and it is in the sky that our flights of fancy take place, before they come crushing to the ground. Signs that appear in the sky—a cross appearing over a battle-field or an advertising banner flying off the tail of a crop duster—are visible to many people and from large distances. The sky illuminates the things that appear in it, revealing them and making them equally accessible to everyone.

In the European political tradition, earth and sky have been set in opposition to each other. This is the *polemos*, the struggle, we have discussed in this chapter—between borders and borderlessness; between the rooted and the unrooted; the local and the universal; home and homelessness. We find the same opposition in international politics: borders, armies and *ragione di stato* belong to the earth; borderlessness, human rights and world government belong to the sky. And it is more than anything the failure to resolve this tension which has brought disaster on us. To conservatives it is obvious that people in modern society spend far too much

---

63 Fried, A Letter to Emmanuel Faye, 244.

time looking up into the sky. Universal values, they argue, are necessarily superficial; the universal belongs to no place in particular, to no person or way of life. This is Chesterton's critique of Kipling and Edmund Burke's critique of the French revolutionaries. "In the groves of their academy, at the end of every vista, you see nothing but the gallows."[64] And yet the greatest crimes of the twentieth-century were surely committed by those who tried to plant themselves most firmly in the ground. By those, that is, who recognized no universal standards. We find the gallows in every *Heimat* too. The search for a *Grund*, a 'foundation', has revealed an *Abgrund*, an 'abyss'.[65]

As we have argued in this chapter, the dichotomy between earth and sky works differently for nomads. For nomads, neither the earth nor the sky are places where you dwell, but both are instead a medium that you pass through in order to get to somewhere else. The sky is infinite but so is the steppe, the desert and the tundra, and in any case the two blend perfectly together at the horizon. As nomadic peoples let us know, there can be order also in a borderless world. There is no rootedness to be sure but also no rootlessness. Life is lived in passing; we carry everything we need with us; we tread lightly on the path that we trace. It is only once we give up the search for a *Grund* that we can avoid the *Abgrund*.

References

Angell, N., *The Great Illusion: A Study of the Military Power to National Advantage*, New York 1913.
Asad, T., "Equality in Nomadic Social Systems?: Notes towards the Dissolution of an Anthropological Category", *Critique of Anthropology*, 3:11 (April 1, 1978), 57–65.
Berman, M., *Wandering God: A Study in Nomadic Spirituality*, 2000.
Bira, S., "Mongolian Tenggerism and Modern Globalism: A Retrospective Outlook on Globalisation", *Inner Asia*, 5: 2 (July 1, 2003), 107–17.
Bollnow, O. F., *Human Space*, translated by Christine Shuttleworth, London 2011.
Burke, E., *Reflections on the Revolution in France: And on the Proceedings in Certain Societies in London Relative to That Event*, London 1790.

---

64 Burke, *Reflections on the Revolution in France*, 115.
65 On these Heideggerian terms, see Mitchell, The Fourfold, 208–18.

Carnegie, A., "The Baseless Fear of War", *The Advocate of Peace*, 75, no. 4 (1913), 79–80.
Carr, E. H., *The Twenty Years' Crisis, 1919–1939: An Introduction to the Study of International Relations*, New York 1964.
Chesterton, G. K., "On Mr. Rudyard Kipling and Making the World Small", in *Heretics*, 38–53, New York 1905.
Davies, W. H., *The Autobiography of a Super-Tramp*, New York 1917.
Diener, A. C./Hagen, J., "City of Felt and Concrete: Negotiating Cultural Hybridity in Mongolia's Capital of Ulaanbaatar", *Nationalities Papers*, 41:4 (July 1, 2013), 622–50.
Eliade, M., *The Sacred and the Profane*, New York 1957.
Ferguson, A., *An Essay on the History of Civil Society*, Edinburgh 1773.
Fitzmaurice, A., "The Genealogy of Terra Nullius", *Australian Historical Studies*, 38:129 (2007), 1–15.
Fried, G., "A Letter to Emmanuel Faye", *Philosophy Today*, 55:3 (2011), 219–252.
Garraty, J. A., "The New Deal, National Socialism, and the Great Depression", *The American Historical Review*, 78:4 (1973): 907–44.
Gibbon, E., *The History of the Decline and Fall of the Roman Empire*, edited by Henry Hart Milman, vol. 3. 6 vols, Boston 1854.
Gilmour, D., *Long Recessional*, New York 2003.
Gong, G. W., *The Standard of 'Civilization' in International Society*, Oxford: 1984.
Harries, K., "Heidegger as a Political Thinker", *The Review of Metaphysics*, 29:4 (June 1976), 642–69.
Hartog, F., *Memories of Odysseus: Frontier Tales from Ancient Greece*, Chicago 2001.
Heidegger, M., *Being and Time*, translated by John Macquarrie and Edward Robinson, New York 1962.
Heidegger, M., "Meßkirch's Seventh Centennial", translated by Thomas J. Sheehan, *Listening*, 8 (1973), 41–57.
Hentilä, S., "The Origins of the Folkhem Ideology in Swedish Social Democracy", *Scandinavian Journal of History*, 3:1–4 (January 1978), 323–45.
Hobbes, T., *Leviathan: The Matter, Forme, & Power of a Common-Wealth Ecclesiasticall and Civill*, London 1651.
Hobsbawm, E. J, *Nations and Nationalism since 1780: Programme, Myth, Reality*, Cambridge 1992.
Ingold, T., *The Perception of the Environment: Essays on Livelihood, Dwelling and Skill*, London 2011.
Kern, S., *The Culture of Time and Space 1880–1918*, Cambridge 1983.
Kradin, N. N, "Nomadism, Evolution and World-Systems: Pastoral Societies in Theories of Historical Development", *Journal of World-Systems Research*, 8:3 (2002), 368–88.
Krell, D. F./Bates, D. L., *The Good European: Nietzsche's Work Sites in Word and Image*, Chicago 1997.
Lemarchand, R., *Forgotten Genocides: Oblivion, Denial, and Memory*, Philadelphia 2011.

Lewis, I. M., *A Pastoral Democracy: Study of Pastoralism and Politics Among the Northern Somali of the Horn of Africa*, Hamburg 1999.
Locke, J., *Two Treatises of Government*, London 1821.
Lorimer, J., *The Institutes of the Law of Nations: A Treatise of the Jural Relations of Separate Political Communities*, vol. 2. 2 vols, Edinburgh 1884.
Lucassen, L., "Eternal Vagrants?: State Formation, Migration and Travelling Groups in Western Europe, 1350–1914", in Leo Lucassen, Wim Willems, and Annemarie Cottaar (eds.), *Gypsies and Other Itinerant Groups: A Socio-Historical Approach*, Basingstoke 1998, 55–73.
MacKay, J./Levin, J./de Carvalho, G./Cavoukian, K./Cuthbert, R., "Before and after Borders: The Nomadic Challenge to Sovereign Territoriality", *International Politics*, 51:1 (January 2014), 101–23.
Martin, D., "On the Cultural Ecology of Sky Burial on the Himalayan Plateau", *East and West*, 46:3/4 (1996), 353–70.
Marx, K./Engels, F., *Manifesto of the Communist Party*, translated by Samuel Moore, Chicago 1910.
Mill, J. S., "Civilization", in *Dissertations and Discussions, Political Philosophical, and Historical. Reprinted Chiefly from the Edinburgh and Westminster Reviews*, Volume I, originally published in 1836, London 1859, 160–205.
Mitchell, A. J., "The Fourfold", in Bret W. Davis (ed.), *Martin Heidegger: Key Concepts*, Durham 2010, 208–18.
Moon, G., *Done and Been: Steel Rail Chronicles of American Hobos*, Bloomington 1996.
Neumann, I. B./Wigen, E., "The Importance of the Eurasian Steppe to the Study of International Relations", *Journal of International Relations and Development*, 16:3 (July 2013), 311–30.
Nietzsche, F., *The Joyful Wisdom* ("La Gaya Scienza"), translated by Thomas Common, New York 1924.
Nugent, J. B./Sanchez, N., "Tribes, Chiefs, and Transhumance: A Comparative Institutional Analysis", *Economic Development and Cultural Change*, 42:1 (1993), 87–113.
Olson, M., *Power And Prosperity: Outgrowing Communist And Capitalist Dictatorships*, New York 2000.
Osterhammel, J., *The Transformation of the World: A Global History of the Nineteenth Century*, translated by Patrick Camiller, Princeton 2014.
Otis, L. C., *Networking: Communicating with Bodies and Machines in the Nineteenth Century*, Ann Arbor 2011.
Podruchny, C., *Making the Voyageur World: Travelers and Traders in the North American Fur Trade*, Lincoln 2006.
Pollard, S., "Free Trade, Protectionism, and the World Economy", in Martin H. Geyer and Johannes Paulmann (eds.), *The Mechanics of Internationalism: Culture, Society, and Politics from the 1840s to the First World War*, Oxford 2001, 27–53.
Ringmar, E., "Heidegger on Willpower and the Mood of Modernity", in Antonio Cerella and Louiza Odysseos (eds.), *Heidegger and the Global Age*, Lanham 2017.

Ringmar, E., "'How to Fight Savage Tribes': The Global War on Terror in Historical Perspective", *Terrorism and Political Violence*, 25:2 (March 2013), 264–83.

Ringmar, E., *Liberal Barbarism: The European Destruction of the Palace of the Emperor of China*, New York 2013.

Ringmar, E., *Political Theory for Nomads*, Cambridge forthcoming.

Ringmar, E., *Surviving Capitalism: How We Learned to Live with the Market and Remained Almost Human*, London 2005.

Ringmar, E., "The Anti-Nomadic Bias of Political Theory", edited by Jamie Levin, Basingstoke forthcoming.

Ringmar, E., "The Great Wall of China Does Not Exist", in Agnese Horvath and Marius Benţa (eds.), *Walling, Boundaries and Liminality: A Political Anthropology of Transformations*, London forthcoming.

Schulze, H., *States, Nations and Nationalism: From the Middle Ages to the Present*, Malden: Wiley-Blackwell 1998.

Seed, P., *Ceremonies of Possession in Europe's Conquest of the New World, 1492–1640*, Cambridge 1995.

Smith, A., *An Inquiry into the Nature and Causes of the Wealth of Nations, vol. 1*, 2 vols, London: Printed for W. Strahan and T. Cadell, in the Strand, 1776.

Sneath, D., *The Headless State: Aristocratic Orders, Kinship Society, & Misrepresentations of Nomadic Inner Asia*, 2007.

Spektorowski, A./Mizrachi, E., "Eugenics and the Welfare State in Sweden: The Politics of Social Margins and the Idea of a Productive Society", *Journal of Contemporary History*, 39:3 (July 1, 2004), 333–52.

Tilly, C., "War Making and State Making as Organized Crime", in Peter Evans, Dietrich Rueschemeyer, and Theda Skocpol (eds.), *Bringing the State Back In*, Cambridge 1985, 169–91.

Tuan, Y.-F., *Space and Place: The Perspective of Experience*, Minneapolis 2001.

Weatherford, J., *Genghis Khan and the Making of the Modern World*, New York 2005.

Weber, E., *Peasants into Frenchmen: The Modernization of Rural France, 1870–1914*, Stanford 1976.

Winichakul, T., *Siam Mapped: A History of the Geo-Body of a Nation*, Honolulu 1997.

Wintrobe, R., "Some Economics of Ethnical Capital Formation and Conflict", in Albert Breton (ed.), *Nationalism and Rationality*, Cambridge 1995, 43–70.

Diplomacy as Global Governance

Iver B. Neumann and Ole Jacob Sending

Introduction

Global order is often seen as centering on the states system, and consisting of a shared set of emergent and contested practices about what the system's units—states—can do, to whom, when and how. The anchoring or framing of global order is seen as sovereignty; the principle that there is no institution above that of states that can ultimately make a state do what it would otherwise not have done. As to agency in the system, we find this in a number of places, but one institution, diplomacy, has emerged as the processual master institution of global order. Our approach to world order here, then, is a fairly conventional one: We assume that order is about relative stability of interaction patterns. Such stability could have all kinds of sources, but at the heart of world order, we assume that we still find the states system, and that diplomacy is at the heart of the states system. Given these assumption, a key question becomes how diplomacy is changing. In order to answer that question, we draw on previous work[1] where we have argued that the state itself is changing, as it goes from working mostly *on* society (by streaming possibilities, giving orders, denying options, taxing etc.), to working increasingly *through* society (by conducting their conduct in terms of incentives, after-the-fact reports, indirect control etc.). We take Norway as our case, because we know it best, but also because Norway, as a small state with an open economy, has a lot to gain from a high degree of world order, and so is spending considerable diplomatic resources on system management and, as we will try to demonstrate, innovation. Given how the tension between state system and humanity is central to questions of world order (see Walker in this volume), we make changes in this particular area the focus of our inquiry. What we find is that, particularly since the end of the Cold War, Norwegian diplomacy has increasingly

---

[1] Neumann and Sending, *Governing the Global Polity*.

worked not only with other Foreign Ministries, but also with and through a number of other agents.

Specifically, Norwegian diplomacy has gone from being less representational—as in representing Norway and its positions on specific issues—to more governmental—as in trying to order chunks of humanity outside Norway's boundaries as a tool to establish order, and to build up political capital vis a vis other states. There is anecdotal evidence to the effect that this point may be generalised to other states, particularly in Northern Europe but also in the West generally and perhaps also more widely. We cannot make scope a key concern here, but we can suggest that something that resembles processes in early states building is now afoot on the global level. One will recall that Émile Durkheim argued that state building was a process of a state cadre opening ever new interfaces with society, so that the two merged in an ever larger degree. Our argument is that we may observe how this process is now bursting the boundaries of states, as some states are opening interfaces with chunks of societies beyond them. Our aim here is not to discuss the pros and cons of such a development, but simply to document that it is afoot. The relevance for this volume is that a world where states take an increasing interest in ordering societal stuff that lies outside its own state boundaries, is a world that is increasingly ordered differently than a world based on the principle of sovereignty.[2] Put differently, if states are increasingly active beyond the states system, then that must mean that global governance is on the rise and that the states system's relation to global order at large is undergoing some very interesting change.

It should be stressed at the outset that we are discussing a transformation, as opposed to a shift. It is not the case that diplomacy has up until recently been exclusively representational, for there has by necessity always been an element of governance in diplomacy. States have collaborated about maintaining their preponderance in global politics, they have collaborated about evolving diplomatic practices and they are continuously tussling about the rules of application that should pertain to those practices.[3] Our point is simply that the element of global governance in diplomatic work is on the rise: we are seeing an intensification of the interfaces between and governmental efforts between and within states through diplomatic work. The result is a world where each sovereign's

---

2 cf. Wendt, Why a World State is Inevitable.
3 Hurd, International Law; Mitzen, From Representation to Governing.

diplomatic work conditions the sovereignty of the other through efforts to govern on one another's territory to different degrees.[4] If we can make such a shift seem probably, we have identified a factor of change in global order, away from a system built on sovereignty towards one where sovereignty is but one of a larger set of competing registers for governance.

A word on how diplomacy is generally conceived in the literature seems in order. Diplomacy is charged with maintaining order, or, to put it more technically, systems maintenance, but given that order consists of practices and practices are changing, it follows that diplomacy itself must also be changing. This is often seen as implying that diplomacy is merely codifying practices that happen elsewhere after the fact. We contest such a reading. While it is true that the problems that diplomacy deals with originate outside of diplomacy itself, it is when diplomacy is brought to bear on these problems that the practices which constitute the part of global order pertaining to the states system come into play. As diplomacy plays itself out, it not only maintains these practices. It also changes them. Over the long haul, and often unwillingly, diplomats and diplomacy comes to deal with new problems in innovative ways. It follows that diplomacy is constitutive of global order, and not only reflective of it, as most scholars seem to assume.

We need not make assumptions about anarchy to see that the institutionalization or centralization of political power in the international system is weak. Rather, we need simply to register that diplomacy is basically about representing one polity vis-à-vis another. To the extent that there is no political authority above these polities, the ways in which diplomacy produces order must involve some type of uncoordinated coordination.

We will try to do this by thinking about diplomacy in terms of power. Drawing on extant work on the emergence of global governmental reason[5], we focus on how diplomatic practice is involved in producing, interpreting and responding to events that are somehow 'problematic'. Obvious cases are war and humanitarian disasters, both of which introduce contingency and unpredictability, where diplomatic practice takes on a distinct role and representation is replaced by governing.

---

4 Onuf, A Constructivist Manifesto.
5 Bartelson, *Sovereignty as Symbolic Form*; Neumann and Sending, *Governing the Global Polity*; Joseph, The Social in the Global.

Power[6]

At a minimum, power is about getting an agent to do something that agent would not otherwise have done. When an agent tries to make another follow a norm, or when two agents try to impose different norms as a framework for action in a given situation, we are talking about a power-laden situation. Diplomacy pertains to certain ways of doing this. These ways change historically. We will try to capture change in global order by identifying changes in diplomacy, and the way we will do it is to draw on the idea that power can take different and changing forms. Specifically, we will employ Michel Foucault's tripartite take on modes of power: sovereignty, dominance and governmentality.[7] Dominance will not concern us further here, as it does not pertain to diplomacy.

Sovereignty is a game of strategic relations between different wills, where it is not clear who is the master. It is this type of power relations—understood as an ongoing negotiation between subjects regarding who is right and who can dictate the other person's actions. The strategic game between different sovereigns (first the King himself, then the states understood as collective sovereign subjects) has been the typical form of power in the European state system. The establishment of the state system from the late 13th century and onwards is inextricably linked to the increase in relations between sovereigns, built on what has later been called sovereignty. Sovereignty can be understood exactly as a strategic game, but one where there are no built-in restrictions hindering dominance to be utilised as a complementary power strategy.

Governmentality is a type of power relation which is connected to the reflexive—that is; how the self governs itself. It is to do with the conduct of conduct, with governing indirectly. Today, there exists a dense network of liberal norms that shapes the identities and behavioural patterns of states. It may be seen as a global system of indirect forms of power that operates to guide, shape and foster specific types of not only states, but also other polities, as well as individuals. It sets up standards of behaviour for individuals and models of institutions to be implemented and followed by all good members of the international community. Jens Bartelson has noted that we "live in a world in which territorial differentiation into distinct nation-states is being challenged by a functional differentiation into

---

6 This section draws on Neumann and Sending (2010).
7 See particularly Foucault, Governmentality, 219, and L'éthique du souci, 728.

distinct issue areas," and that "the sovereign equality of states no longer constitutes the baseline for further stratification according to relative strength and power. In this world, there are several normative frameworks competing for both legality and legitimacy when it comes to justifying political practices, such as intervention"[8].

There is a tension here. On the one hand, global order is traditionally seen as resting on sovereign dynamics between territorially defined polities. On the other hand, global order is increasingly marked by the tensions between and political dynamics ensuing over different governmental rationalities of order. This is our point of entry, for if diplomacy is an integral part of the emergence of competing rationalities of rule existing side-by-side with territorially defined polities, then the workings of diplomacy will reflect those changes.

That we conceive of power in this way has implications for how we should understand diplomacy as a practice through which order—and transformation—is continually produced and reproduced. As an infrastructure through which states both represent and engage in governing beyond its borders, diplomacy pulls together a range of tools and actors to engage in governing. Because diplomacy is the default setting for the engagement with other states, non-state actors tend to mimic diplomatic practices even when such actors seek to challenge established political practice. And because diplomats arguably do claim a level of jurisdictional control over such engagement with other states, they are able to 'diplomaticize' how non-diplomats perform their tasks when they engage in governing. Examples include how advocacy networks tailor their strategies in ways that conform to established diplomatic practices at multilateral negotiations, how they set up embassy-like offices in countries where they operate, and how diplomatic skills emerge as central to actors that engage in, say, military liaison and advice functions[9] and in development and humanitarian work[10].

In this context, we can think of diplomacy as a practice that other actors, by dint of globalization, mimic and emulate as they, too, increasingly operate on other states territory. Diplomats, for their part, seek to enrol and govern on other states territories through these actors as they move beyond representation. The result is that diplomacy entails a significant

---

[8] Bartelson, The Concept of Sovereignty Revisited, 474.
[9] Krieger, Nouma and Nexon, US military diplomacy in practice.
[10] Sending, Diplomats and Humanitarians.

element of assembling and pulling together a wide array of tools and actors, and when codified, tend to diffuse to of new areas. This means that diplomacy is a practice through which order is produced and transformed. Let us now turn to diplomatic practice in order to inquire whether, and in which degree, we may trace a shift in global order from resting on sovereign norms to resting on governmental norms.

Changes in Diplomatic Practice

We may say that we are dealing with a situation where the decision on what constitutes an 'exception' is no longer the state's to make. Rather, what constitutes an exception is highly regulated by international norms and practices. In Bartelson's formulation, the implication is that the "competences previously thought to be integral to statehood have been vested in the international community"[11]. He continues to reflect on what this implies for our understanding of the international system:

"The international system cannot be expected to regulate itself and correct its own imbalances spontaneously through traditional institutions such as diplomacy, international law, and balance of power. Rather, since the international system is prone to disorder, not primarily because of rivalries between states, but because of the constant risk that state dysfunction might spill over into system dysfunction, then the governmentalization of sovereignty is a way to maintain international order, as well as conversely. Thus the *continuity and viability of the international system depend on an array of maintenance functions carried out by a variety of non-state actors.* [...] [A] global civil society now functions as the main conveyor belt of governmentalization and hence also as an important mechanism for monitoring and regulating the international system. As a result, the international system now appears less as a natural kind or as a social construct, and more as a holographic projection of a globalized will to govern"[12].

This is in keeping with our own previous work, where we have suggested that the 'international' has become governmentalized in important respects.[13] But both our own past work on this, as well as Bartelson's work, have arguably skirted the issue of how such a governmentalization of the

---

11 Bartelson, Sovereignty, 2092 Kindle.
12 Ibid., 2092–2122 Kindle.
13 Neumann and Sending, 'The International'.

international system, and of sovereignty, has spawned important changes in diplomatic practice. In other words: if the international system is now increasingly structured by maintenance functions that are distinct from conventional diplomatic practice, then we would expect to find changes in the very functioning of diplomacy as well. And indeed, as we will see shortly, diplomacy has evolved to include a heavy emphasis on the managing of disorder that stem not from inter-state conflict but from intra-state breakdown. Such management of disorder has increasingly become a staple of diplomacy. Diplomacy is itself becoming a distinct governmental rationality—organized around the management of relationships rather than managing disorder—and so we have a case of hybridization of diplomatic practices that draw on different registers, some of which are traditional diplomatic ones, some of which are borrowed from humanitarian relief work, and others which are taken from the model of a neutral mediator or umpire in the conflicts of others. Taken together, we see that these new practices, which are geared towards managing and preventing disorder, are integrated within diplomatic institutions in such a way that they are instrumentalized and used principally for more traditional 'diplomatic' ends such as status seeking.[14]

Since we are looking for change, we choose to look at two relatively new diplomatic practice fields, namely peace and reconciliation and humanitarian disaster relief. These are both focused on situations that are exceptional, prompting a particular type or style of diplomatic work that is widespread. This diplomatic work is distinct from regular, non-exceptional diplomatic work. The differentiation of the new practices from regular diplomatic work is of key importance, for it tells us something about the multiple and heterogeneous orders produced through diplomatic work.

The Diplomacy of Peace and Reconciliation

It is a defining trait of a state system that certain states act as a so-called third party, lending its so-called good offices to alleviate conflict between other states. In fact, being able to fill this role was a defining trait of 18th century great powers. For example, it was a milestone for Russia on its way

---

14 de Carvalho and Neumann, *Small State Status-Seeking*.

to this status when it was allowed, in 1779, to mediate the Treaty of Teschen that ended the War of the Bavarian Succession between Austria and Prussia. Brokerage—active participation in crisis management and/or long-term trust-building—would be one form of third party activity. Another and weaker form is facilitation, where a state offers its services not as an active broker, but as a discreet presence with certain human and material resources to offer. In fact, facilitation and brokerage are not readily disentangled. Suffice it to say that, as is the case with the distinction between military operations and peace operations, the difference hinges on structural factors, such as the military capability of the polity in question, with centrally placed polities being more associated with brokerage than with facilitation.

During last century, there emerged a sizeable community of organizations in Geneva and elsewhere that specialize in facilitation, converging on organizations such as the International Committee of the Red Cross (ICRC) and the Centre for Human Development. States were late to this networked, multi-stakeholder affair, with one interesting feature of post-Cold War politics being how a number of polities have increased the resources allocated to facilitation. The first state to do so was Norway, which made distinct moves in this direction already in the early 1990s. (The Norwegian MFA established a separate section to deal with Peace and Reconciliation in 2004.) Other states now regularly seek out Norway to discuss doing something similar, but to date, Ireland is the only other state that has actually institutionalized facilitation as part of its diplomacy. Several other MFAs are now stepping up their efforts in peace and reconciliation. Examples include a Finnish–Swedish joint proposal to establish a European Union Institute for Peace and a joint Finnish–Turkish announcement that they will work to strengthen the UN's work in this area.[15]

Here we have one possible transformative change in diplomatic practice: Mediation goes from being an inter-state to being a multiple-actor affair. State diplomacy, which used to turn on the mediation of bilateral or multilateral state-to-state relations, begins to occupy itself directly with what is happening inside a state. There are two sides to this equation: who is doing the mediation and between whom that mediation is carried out. We do not see any systems-transforming potential when mediators use

---

15 Ministry for Foreign Affairs of Finland, Peace Mediation – *Finland's Guidelines*.

sub-state agents from their own society. The argument against this being a systems-transforming aspect is a straightforward one, and comes in two different flavors of power realism. There is, first, the principal agent argument. If the state delegates something to another agent that is nested within it, then the resulting agency is a delegated one, and what is delegated can be revoked.[16] Realists tend to subscribe to this argument. The other route along which to arrive on the same conclusion is that it is the state which always draws the line between what is a state concern and what is a society concern.[17] By simply manipulating the line between these two entities, the state may revoke any privileges previously granted.[18]

As we will see, however, states are now also drawing on sub-state actors which do *not* hail from their own society. By the same logic that cancels the importance of the use of sub-state agents from their own societies, the use of non-national NGOs is significant, for these non-principal agents will be primarily responsive to the state where they are based, as opposed to the mediating state in a third-party role that is drawing on its services. For this reason and others, it will be that much harder for the delegating agent to muster resources to keep the non-principal agents inline. The diplomatic use of such actors is not historically new, but during the heyday of nationalism, it was a waning practice. Its return is, therefore, significant.

We also want to highlight the other side of the equation of mediation, namely what kind of actors the third party is mediating between. The point here is that third parties are increasingly mediating not between states, but between a state apparatus that is threatened by another polity on what it considers its own territory. Consider our case, Norway, and its mediation effort in Sri Lanka, between the government, clearly ethnically Sinhalese, and the ethnically distinct guerilla organization known as the Tamil Tigers. This facilitating experience was definitely formative for Norwegian diplomatic practice, for it spelled a need to separate the state-to-state work done by embassies abroad and desks at home from peace and reconciliation work. As one former head of section pointed out in an interview, if the job of the facilitator is to find out where different parties to a conflict stand and bring those two parties to the table, then a neutral

---

16 Kiewiet and McCubbins, *The Logic of Delegation*.
17 Mitchell, *Colonising Egypt*.
18 For a book-length argument of how this means that the state will not necessarily be weakened by globalization, see Neumann and Sending, *Governing the Global Polity*.

approach is called for. When one of those parties would be a state, and the other not, as was the case in Sri Lanka, such an approach is the diametrically opposite of the state-focused approach of bilateral diplomacy, which has as its main job to work with the host government.[19] The practices involved—and by practices we simply mean "socially recognized forms of activity, done on the basis of what members learn from others, and capable of being done well or badly, correctly or incorrectly"—are very different, and cluster around four logically consecutive (but not easily disentangible) situations or steps.[20] These are mapping the parties to a conflict, clearing their path to the table, assisting in their deliberations going across that table and, finally, being indirectly involved in the monitoring of any agreement being struck.

Step one of peace and reconciliation work is to develop contacts with all parties involved, indeed with as wide a group of societal agents as possible. For Norway, this process sped up in the early 1990s. In the Oslo Process, they came through a trade union think tank doing humanitarian work in the region (FAFO). In Guatemala and Ethiopia, and also in Mali, they came through Norwegian Church Aid (Loder 1997).[21] In the Sudan, a number of Norwegian NGOs which were involved in development

---

19 Interview with former head of section, 9 July 2010.
20 Barnes, Practice as Collective Action, 19.
21 Loder, The Peace Process in Mali. Particularly in Guatemala, Norwegian state action was crucial. As noted by the Canadian ambassador to Guatemala at the time, "[the first Norwegian ambassador Fredrik]Arthur opened the office, [his successor]Arne Aasland came down, and that was it. The Norwegian NGOs were good, we had a lot of informal contacts with them, and they had contacts with the military. The Canadians [NGOs] didn't have that, they were of the Vietnam generation and ideological purity was more important to them than getting the thing moving. Norwegian NGOs were not like that. I remember Asbjørn Eide came to a seminar in Canada and we [DFAIT] were clashing with the Human Rights activists from the NGOs, it was really bad, and Eide said [to the Canadian NGOs] you are 10 years behind the Norwegian NGOs. By that, he meant that the Norwegians were keeping their eyes on the job. They [Norwegian diplomats] would invite people from the military, and then the guerrillas over to chat, soften them up, with a view to making them sit down together. The first meetings are not usually very productive in such cases. Arne would have them over to his own home in Oslo. Colombia was the same. One problem would be that that they would be suspicious of Norway's motives. Arne told me they would ask "do you have a petroleum thing coming or something". Interview with Dan Livermore, DFAIT, former Canadian Ambassador to Guatemala, Waterloo, 29 September 1999.

furnished the contacts, whereas in Sri Lanka, it was basically one former politician's network that got the ball rolling.[22]

The Norwegian efforts in this direction, which, as we have seen, gave the impulse to institutionalization within the Norwegian MFA, also had a certain path dependence on the international level. As already noted, besides the UN in New York, the main focal point for peace and reconciliation work internationally is Geneva, and the most important actor based in Geneva is the ICRC. It was therefore anything but surprising that, when Norwegian Foreign Minister Stoltenberg recruited a Norwegian to develop the peace and reconciliation portfolio at the MFA, he handpicked a person who was working at the ICRC's headquarters in Geneva. To this list we should add the Centre for Humanitarian Dialogue, in Geneva, a private Swiss entity with funding from a range of governments and non-governmental sources. Established in 1999 to pick up cases that the International Committee of the Red Cross (ICRC) cannot pursue given its mandate, it is involved in a range of mediation efforts across the world.

The institutionalization of peace and conflict work at the international level means that, once a certain agent is involved, it becomes privy to information on a whole plethora of different conflicts that is more or less freely shared. The symbiotic relations that ensue between a state like Norway and the ICRC and other agents in Geneva means not only that information on new conflicts and overtures to Norway about playing a facilitating role in new conflicts will ensue, but also that Norway becomes involved in a gift economy where certain services will at some time have to be set against certain others. Note also that this kind of symbiosis means that the diplomacy pursued by Norway must necessarily involve non-state agents, and so be transformative of diplomacy itself. In the succinct analysis of one former head of section:

"Our [i.e. Norway's] contacts with the ICRC and the cooperation we have developed with the Centre for Humanitarian Dialogue in Geneva are parts of a greater whole [...] Operating together with a private actor makes so many things so much easier. They have easier access to all parties involved. Once states are seen to enter the fray, it all becomes more serious; stakes increase and deniability

---

22 Since the Oslo Accords were signed in 1993, Norway has been officially facilitating in Guatemala, Sri Lanka, the Sudan, the Middle East, Colombia, the Philippines, Timor-Leste, Haiti, Burundi, Eritrea, Mali, Nepal, Cyprus and the West Balkans, and unofficially in Spain (the Basque country).

decreases. As the process matures, however, there usually comes a time when you [i.e. the parties to the process] need services that only a state can provide in order to clinch the process. For example, a state is a much more credible witness, it offers much better security services and it can bring stuff to the table that others often cannot, such as territory. I think we have a school for new diplomacy here, in the sense that this is a new way of working. When we talk to states, we often cannot penetrate beyond their presentations of the general line. We get more of the static (*vi får mye mer av støyen*). By working with a whole gamut of actors and not only states, we come closer to the gist of the political. It is interesting to see how the private actors we work with used to be Norwegians only, but now we use whoever is handy."[23]

When a conflict is diplomatized, it changes the conflict, but it also changes diplomacy, in two principal ways. The object of state diplomacy goes from being another state to being all the agents that are relevant to a certain conflict, state or otherwise. Furthermore, instead of drawing only on the society which an MFA ostensibly represents, the MFA draws on a whole plethora of agents which do *not* hail from its own society in its work:

"We work a lot with CHD, for they have tailor-made expertise on mediation, but also with Jonathan Powell, Interpeace, Conciliation Resources, International peace Institute, Centre for International Cooperation at the N[ew] Y[ork] U[niversity] and so on. In addition to building up our own expertise and consolidate the Section, I think of us as a kind of administrative hub on managing different peace processes."[24]

This amounts to no less than a decentering of diplomacy, where traditional bilateral and multilateral state-oriented diplomacy gives way to networking.[25] It turned out that the subject matter engaged in—desecuritization—changed the face of diplomacy by changing the way it had to be conducted; less state-to-state, more networked.

If step one of a facilitator's work is mapping the parties in terms of political structure and political views, step two is to nudge the parties in the direction of dialogue. This may be done by indirect means, by initiating or bending already existing frameworks in the margins of which the parties may meet. One example of such a framework would be a religious dialogue. Such efforts will have to be preceded by direct contacts, however. Whereas the state side to a conflict usually controls territory and has the

---

23 Interview with former head of section, 9 July 2010.
24 Interview with head of section, 4 June 2012.
25 Neumann, At Home with the Diplomats.

accompanying freedom of maneuver that comes with such control, for other parties the physical security aspects of surfacing may loom large. The non-state parties take a risk by surfacing. Even if a number of intermediaries are used, they incur a substantial risk simply by talking to facilitators, meaning that facilitators have to be utterly discreet. One former head of section made a comment in this regard which strikes to the heart of diplomats' self-understanding. Highlighting the covert aspect of operations, the following point was made: "This is why peace and reconciliation work is found at the interstice of diplomacy and intelligence. It is imperative, however, that diplomats take care of this, since the intelligence people always have a double agenda. They also want to know who they might have to kill."[26]

It is the understanding of this diplomat, and, we would add, of diplomats generally, that they have a firm commitment to the diplomatization of conflict. This is in keeping with how professions are defined by efforts to establish and maintain jurisdictional control over certain tasks.[27] Other professions involved, and particularly the military, are seen by diplomats as having a double agenda, always asking themselves the question of whether diplomatization or violisation of the conflict may bring about what they at any one given time hold to be the optimal course of action. It must also be said, however, that the diplomatic self-understanding differs from what one learns from the historical record on this point, for diplomats themselves were, and still are, also prone to consider moves other than de-securitising ones.

Once the parties have agreed to talk, a third facilitating step would be to bring them physically to the table. This involves finding, and often paying for, spaces where the parties may meet in a secure and relaxed atmosphere conducive to work and trust-building. This is delicate stuff, for if the setting is too reclusive, the ties between negotiators and their constituencies become weaker, and a lot of time-consuming shuttling between negotiators and (the rest of) the leadership will tend to ensue. The facilitator needs a light touch at this point, for on the one hand there will always be incentives to speed up the process, whereas on the other hand, too much rush may bring the dialogue tumbling down.

The facilitator's work may end at this stage, but it may also involve a fourth step, namely monitoring of the agreements reached. Again, this is

---

26 Interview with former head of section, 9 July 2010.
27 Sending, *The Politics of Expertise*. Abbott, *The Systems of Professions*.

risky business, for as pointed out by a former head of the section, "[f]acilitators of a certain deal should not become the umpires of that deal. Facilitation and monitoring should be treated as two discreet functions".[28]

There are a number of indications in extant literature that supports this diplomat's sense that we are looking at a major shift in diplomatic practices. For example, already in 1986, John Vincent discussed the issue of human rights, and found a systems-transforming potential. Human rights are thought from the individual, not the state, but they are handled by states and so make up a potentially disruptive subject of international relations. Vincent advanced the argument that attempts to resolve the clash between an inherent rights logic and the logic which dominated the working of the states system seemed to focus crucially on the institution of international law, where a body of what is called *ius gentium intra se* is being worked out. This body of law regulates the boundary and working of a bundle of human rights defined as a common concern to states, the violation of which may lead to a humanitarian intervention being launched. Diplomats, Vincent argued, had to find ways of dealing with this new subject matter.[29] He also argued that to the extent that they succeed, this would boost systems maintenance (or, in his terms, international society).

Diplomats have found such ways, not only regarding human rights, but also regarding peace and reconciliation work. Note, first, that the demand for such work comes from state and non-state agents that experience a need for help; it is a ground rule of facilitation that it should only be given when both parties to the conflict want it. Note also that this work takes the diplomats involved away from the representational and towards the governmental; the primary job is to restore and regulate social order. Representational diplomacy remains important. Norway uses peace and reconciliation work to gain access to great power leaders, to profile Norway as a peace nation, to demonstrate agency to its own population etc. It would be downright silly to conclude that old diplomatic practices do not assert themselves in this issue area. The point we set out to make, however, is that diplomacy is increasingly *also* (as opposed to alternatively) about governance. As for peace and reconciliation work, this is definitely the case. We now turn to another diplomatic issue area, namely humanitarian disaster relief, to see if we may find a similar development there.

---

28 Interview with former head of section, 9 July 2010.
29 Vincent, *Human Rights and International Relations*.

The Diplomacy of Humanitarian Disaster Relief

The interest of peace and reconciliation work for our purposes lies in how it has become something that states do together with non-state agents that do not reside within their territory, and how the practice targets not state-to-state conflict, but conflict between a state and another political agent within it. Diplomacy has evolved new practices, but within an already established field (facilitation and mediation of conflict). Humanitarian disaster relief, on the other hand, is not a traditional field of diplomatic activity at all. Humanitarianism is an old idea, though, and since the Second World War, it has become the key frame for categorizing and acting on conflicts and natural disasters.[30] The expansion of UN peace operations since the 1990s and until today has a lot to do with how humanitarian ideals—and in particular the principle of 'protection of civilians'—have become central to international justifications for different ways to intervene in and seek to address violent conflicts.[31]

The alert reader may spot a seeming mismatch between our case studies. When discussing peace and reconciliation, we included what happens at the receiving end of diplomats' work—facilitation is global governance in the degree that it reduces a presumably sovereign government to a party more or less on a par with some rebel group, and then treats the relation between these two subjects as something that needs external governance. In our discussions of humanitarian disaster relief, however, we will simply take it for granted that a state which harbors, or has created, a crisis on its territory, or that is not able to deal efficiently with a natural disaster by following national standard operational procedures, but which needs help from IOs and NGOs, is at the receiving end of global governance. Most recently, in Nepal, the government was not even able to stop criminal elements from cordoning off Katmandu airport to the very same IOs and NGOs that the Nepalese government had itself invited. It was left to those IOs and NGOs themselves to pay their way into the state in order to help.

We see little point in dwelling on how it is the logic of global governance, and not the logic of sovereignty, that characterizes such overall situations, for we think it should be obvious that state sovereignty did not characterize this situation. If a humanitarian crisis is an exception, and

---

30 Barnett, *Empire of Humanity*.
31 Orford, *International Authority*.

if he is sovereign who decides over the exception, then the very presence of diplomats on such scenes goes to demonstrate that we have a situation of global governance, and not one of state sovereignty qua representation.[32]

Another difference between our two cases is that, in the case of peace and reconciliation, diplomats themselves are on the ground. In the case of humanitarian disaster relief, however, diplomats become involved at a distance. Our job here is to in this article is to demonstrate how diplomatic work becomes global governance work, and so it follows logically that the focus has to be on diplomatic work where it happens, be that at home or away. So, what may seem like a mismatch to the indiscriminating eye, turns out to be a logical consequence of our choice of research focus.

The Norwegian MFA's involvement with humanitarian work remained formally non-existent until after the Second World War, but, when state sovereignty was conferred upon it in 1905, the entire Norwegian foreign policy discourse was rooted in humanitarian thinking.[33] Still, there did exist dense networks between people doing humanitarian work and Norwegian diplomats. Diplomats were not officially in this work, but they knew about it, and many took an interest as it were in a private capacity.

During the Cold War, humanitarian work of all stripes was treated as part of a wider development complex which was organized in a separate directorate and coordinated by the MFA's Second Political Section. In 1997, the latter initiated a split of the section into a Section for Human Rights and a Section for Humanitarian Aid. According to the last head of the section before the split, the terms used were not too specific at this time:

"We always spoke about humanitarian development. [...] We authorized the UN to take care of it all (*gav dem* in blanco-*fullmakt*). There could be an earthquake in the morning, and in the evening we could say that Norway is already helping out. [...] We listened to the High Commissioner [for Refugees]. We gave them a lot of money for blankets and the like, so when we heard on the radio that Norway did its part, it was not because we had been particularly clever [...] We also had very close ties to the NGOs."[34]

All the interviewees confirmed this larger picture. According to the first head of section,

---

32 Mitzen, From Representation to Governing.
33 Knutsen, Leira and Neumann, *Norsk utenrikspolitikks idehistorie*.
34 Telephone interview, 12 September 2014.

"we worked very reactively [...] Money to humanitarian crises was capital for the [MFA's] politicians. The payments happened very quickly so that politicians could say that 'we are now sending x to country y'. One example would be the secretary of state who was on her way to Mozambique and said she needed us to make a payment. We thought she was talking about applications and so on, but she expected the deed to have been done when she landed there the next day."[35]

The same interviewee reported on the detrimental consequences for one's reputation when this style of work clashed with a general professional ethos of the diplomat as a doer[36]: "The one who digs up money will often be seen simply as a cashier".[37] A senior diplomat who had served in the section previously, referred to it as "a till".[38] A recent head of section confirmed this picture in describing the style of work as follows:

"The budget now stands at NOK 3 billion, an all-time high and around 10 per cent of the overall development budget. When the humanitarian budget is ready at the beginning of the year, we draw up priority document (*prioriteringsnotat*), complete with a reserve, and present it to the political leadership. All our case handlers have direct contacts into the UN system. Appeals keep coming. The newly implemented UN system of dividing crises into three levels is a help. At present, four crises rated as level three crises: South Sudan, CAR, Syria, Iraq. A level three status activates a certain coordinating system, releases personnel and money and also calls for more analysis. When the UN appeals to us specifically, we usually respond. [...] We also have appeals from national and international NGOs."[39]

In contrast to many other comparable foreign ministries, such as the Swedish and Danish ones, Norwegian humanitarian funding is *not* placed in a development directorate, but in the foreign ministry proper. The humanitarian funding is, as one informant put it,

"used to advance broader Norwegian interests: We have given priority to Sudan, Afghanistan, Palestine and so on, because we have had interests beyond humanitarian ones. Of course, the modality of offering humanitarian assistance is in keeping with humanitarian principles (neutrality, impartiality and so on), but we have always linked funding decisions to political interests."[40]

---

35 Interview, 4 September 2014, Oslo.
36 See Neumann, *At Home with the Diplomats*.
37 Interview, 4 September 2014, Oslo.
38 Interview, 14 August 2014, Oslo.
39 Interview, 31 October 2014, Oslo.
40 Interview B, 13 January, 2015, New York.

The linking of humanitarian aims to political interests is one that, for the MFA, appears self-evident and unproblematic. It is a testament to how the quest for agency on the part of the Norwegian state shapes the articulation and use of humanitarian funds: it is used selectively to invest in humanitarian relief in some countries that are considered important for Norwegian interests overall. These 'interests' are process-oriented, as humanitarian funding is seen as a ticket to meetings and arenas where Norway would otherwise not have had access, such as the Quartet that coordinates assistance to Palestinian Authorities, the position that Norway has established on Sudan /South Sudan, and also in Afghanistan.[41]

To put it bluntly, the diplomacy of disaster relief is explicitly also about increasing Norway's presence and standing within these specific networks of global governance. As in the case of peace and reconciliation, the representational aspect of diplomacy—being there—remains important. Note, and this is a key point for our undertaking, that the perceived need for representation is not in any way annulled by the growth in global governance. As seen from the state, global governance networks are, among other things, new arenas for diplomatic representation and competition for status.[42]

The increase in political use of disaster relief spelled a need for more coordination between diplomats working within this subfield and other diplomats. During the 1990s, and up until the war in Afghanistan, the Humanitarian Section in the Norwegian MFA typically operated solo, and did not coordinate much with other sections in the Ministry, be that with embassies or desks at home. With the war in Afghanistan, however, this changed:

"We were used to operating a bit like humanitarian cowboys and operated on the idea that we should save lives first and ask questions later. But our involvement in the war in Afghanistan prompted public debates about the military profile of the operation, and we worked to detail Norway's 'total contribution' to Afghanistan, including humanitarian aid. We had to sit down with other sections and work it out. It was far from frictionless, but we did it and now there is a much better coordination with regional desks and also others within the Ministry."[43]

The issue here was not only the fact that humanitarian relief was allocated to Afghanistan, but that it was targeted to certain areas and activities in

---

41 Interview B, 13 January, 2015, New York.
42 De Carvalho and Neumann, Small State Status-Seeking.
43 Interview B, 13 January, 2015, New York.

Afghanistan that were aligned with the Provincial Reconstruction Team (PRT) that Norwegian forces were part of: "This became a very contested issue, with concerns that Norwegian humanitarian aid became a tool to win hearts and minds".[44]

Beyond the use of humanitarian aid in particular conflicts or where Norway has a particular interest, the way humanitarian funds are allocated and through what channels is of importance for our discussion. Humanitarian aid is allocated through large, often Norwegian, humanitarian NGOs with which the MFA has a so-called Framework Agreement, and also through the Central Emergency Response Fund (CERF), a UN coordinated relief fund that is used to disperse funds quickly, before a so-called 'Consolidated Appeals Process' (CAP) has been performed to solicit funds for a particular crisis. The allocation of funds is made early in each calendar year, and the whole section is engaged in producing the 'Allocation Document' (*Fordelingsnotatet*) in January. This key document spells out which countries/crises that will receive funding and which organizations that will handle what. About 15% is kept in reserve every year for contingencies. The bulk of funding goes either to three large humanitarian NGOs in Norway with which the MFA has a framework agreement, or to UN agencies, such as United Nations High Commissioner for Refugees (UNHCR) and the UN Secretariat's Office for the Coordination of Humanitarian Affairs (OCHA).

The humanitarian work of the MFA was subject to two external reviews in 2005/2006. The OECD DAC initiated a peer review process of Norwegian humanitarian aid in 2005. This review pointed to a number of limitations, including the relative lack of bureaucratization and a shortage of written documentation for important allocation decisions. This was, according to our informants, not so much a critique of the contents of decisions but of their lack of documentation, in the form of background notes, decision letters etc. The following year, the Auditor General's Office launched an administrative review of how the work of the Section was organized and how it allocated funds. It was noted in both reviews that the decision making procedures lacked proper structure—too much of the Section's work was considered to unplanned and happenstance. Not surprisingly, once the field of humanitarian disaster relief was increasingly made part of global governance, that is, once it was made less about

---

44 Interview B, 13 January, 2015, New York.

exceptions and more about order maintenance, the MFA started to rely more and more on non-state actors to perform core (diplomatic) tasks, such as negotiation access, serving as facilitators and mediators with governments etc.

Even in cases where Norway has an embassy in a country where a humanitarian crisis is happening, the embassy is reportedly relying heavily on the information and expertise of the resident representatives of Norwegian NGOs for information. The close and informal contacts between these NGOs and the MFA also extend to allocation of funds: "When there is a crisis the head of the Norwegian Red Cross would call us [i.e. the humanitarian section of the MFA], or the Foreign Minister, and say that we need money…"[45]. In terms of personnel overlap, there are multiple revolving doors. Perhaps most strikingly, no less than three of the Norwegian Foreign Ministers over the last three decades have also served as Heads of the Norwegian Red Cross.[46] On the level of diplomats, four people who have worked in the humanitarian section of the MFA have also worked in the NGOs that are being funded mainly by the MFA's humanitarian section.

More generally, what we see here is that there is one, and only one, reaction to any crisis, which is to make a payment. There is no knowledge production about what constitutes a crisis within the section itself.[47] How could it be, when knowledge production about humanitarian crises has to be phronetic, while all that is going on within the humanitarian section is technical. What is a crisis is defined outside the section, and outside the MFA, by the UN, an NGO or an MFA politician's own political agenda. As one diplomat who formerly worked in the section reported, "The NGOs—good people, those—were on our tails constantly. And international organisations as well".[48] NGO representatives confirmed this picture: "The louder we shout and the more info we can provide, particularly from theatres of war, the more they [i.e the humanitarian

---

45 InterviewB, 13 January 2015, New York.

46 Note that this cannot be seen as an irregularity, since all national Red Cross/Red Crescent societies are auxiliaries of the Government, established by acts of parliament; see http://www.ifrc.org/en/what-we-do/disaster-management/responding/disaster-response-system/dr-tools-and-systems/red-cross-red-crescent-national-societies/. What we have here is institutionalized governmentality (see Neumann & Sending 2010). The ministers in question are Thorvald Stoltenberg, Jonas Gahr Støre and Børge Brende,

47 Compare Acuto, Diplomats in Crisis.

48 Interview, 13 August 2014, Oslo.

section] listen".[49] We contend that the humanitarian section, and therefore the MFA, certainly acknowledges natural and human-made humanitarian crises, but they cannot be said to engage in crisis management regarding these crises. They take their cue from when to act from others and leave it to those others to engage in crisis management. There is discursive acknowledgement that humanitarian crises exist, but the institutional practices have nothing to do with crisis management. By outsourcing the decisions of when to act as well as the entire process of implementation to other agents, and by doing it in a thoroughly scripted way, the MFA makes certain that diplomats who are working in the humanitarian section are doing global governance full time. Note, however, that it does not follow that the entire field of humanitarian crisis relief is governmentalized, for the overall decision of which areas to give priority to as well as the size of aid still rest with the MFA. As in the case of peace and reconciliation diplomacy, humanitarian crisis diplomacy demonstrates clearly that, while representational practices are still important, the amount of global governance work done by diplomats is increasing.

Conclusion

Diplomacy is usually thought of as representational: Diplomats act on behalf of states. In this way, they lend agency to state relations and maintains the states system. In order to emerge as an institution, diplomacy has seen concerted action by diplomats that cannot be called representational, but must be thought of as cooperative. Throughout the history of the states system, cooperation has strengthened the communicative matrix of states.[50]

In this chapter, we have traced the increase in another kind of diplomatic work, namely work that is done not only in the name of state honour or state interest (representational work), and not only in order to strengthen the matrix of state communication (cooperative work), but in order to maintain the wider global order. Our two examples were peace and reconciliation work and humanitarian relief work. It is not the case that these areas are new to diplomats. The key thing is that, as late as half a

---

49 Interview, Foreign Executive Director of NGO, 21 November 2014, Oslo.
50 Neumann, Diplomacy.

century ago, peace and reconciliation work by states centered on mediating between states, and humanitarian relief was a state-to-state concern. We have demonstrated in some detail that since then, diplomats have come to do a lot of work in these areas that is not state-to-state, but that aims to build global order beyond the states system. In the first case, this is done as states work with international and national NGOs. In the second case, this is done as states work with IOs and NGOs.

The point here is definitely not that states become weaker. On the contrary, by working through international networks, if anything, they become stronger.[51] One could even argue that being able to act in a multiplicity of ways, some of them networked, is exactly what makes states strong in our era. Neither is our point that diplomacy is no longer about state interest. As we have gone out of our way to stress, the representational logic is still strong, and it also asserts itself when states are doing global governance. Status competition between mediating and donor states remains a commonplace phenomenon. The rise of global governance as a concern of diplomats is a complementary development to all that.

We took as our starting point that diplomats work the states system, and we concluded that increasingly, diplomats also work in order to shore up the global system overall. We charted how diplomats are trying to reduce tension and state collapse by mediating in civil war-like environments, and how they are trying to stabilize crises, shore up the spread of decease and rebuild infrastructure after natural and human-made disasters. It is well known that multilateral diplomacy is focused on global governance. What we have tried to demonstrate here is that national Ministries of Foreign Affairs are also increasingly involved in global governance work. At least where peace and reconciliation and humanitarian crisis management are concerned, multi-stakeholder global governance is a state-run show. In the upshot, the states system is opening ever new interfaces to chunks of society globally. The implication for world order is that, as states firm their social foundations globally, the system of states becomes *more* important than before.

---

51 Neumann and Sending, *Governing the Global Polity*.

References

Abbott, A., *The System of Professions*, Chicago 1988.
Acuto, M., "Diplomats in Crisis", *Diplomacy & Statecraft*, 22 (2011), 521–539.
Barnes, B., "Practice as Collective Action", in Schatzky, T., Knorr Cetina, K. and von Savigny, E. (eds.), *The Practice Turn in Contemporary Theory*, London 2001, 17–28.
Barnett, M., *Empire of Humanity: A History of Humanitarianism*, Ithaca, NY 2011.
Bartelson, J., *Sovereignty as Symbolic Form*, London 2014.
Bartelson, J., "The Concept of Sovereignty Revisited", *European Journal of International Law*, 17 (2006), 463–474.
Boltanski, L., *Distant Suffering: Morality, Media and Politics*, Cambridge 1999.
Brende, B., *Statement by Minister of Foreign Affairs of Norway, HE Mr Børge Brende, at the international conference on Syria*. Geneva II. Montreux, 22 January 2014. http://www.norway-geneva.org/humanitarian/Statements/Statement-by-Minister-of-Foreign-Affairs-of-Norway-HE-Mr-Borge-Brende-at-the-international-conference-on-Syria--Geneva-II/#.VMC3ov6G9os, retrieved 2 September 2015.
Calhoun, C., "The Idea of Emergency: Humanitarian Action and Global (Dis)Order", in Fassin, D. and Pandolfi, M. (eds.), *Contemporary States of Emergency*, New York 2010, 29–58.
de Carvalho, B./Neumann, I.B. (eds), *Small State Status Seeking. Norway's Quest for International Standing*. London, 2015.
Durkheim, E., *Professional Ethics and Civic Morals*. Nabu Press [1958] 2011.
Foucault, M., "Governmentality", in Faubion, J. D. (ed.), *Power: Essential Works of Foucault 1954-1984*, Harmondsworth [1978] 2000, 201–22.
Foucault, M., "L'éthique du souci de soi comme pratique de la liberté", in *Dits et écrits (1954–1988)*, Paris 1994, 708–29.
Hurd, I., "International Law and the Politics of Diplomacy", in Sending, O. J., Pouliot, V. and Neumann, I. B. (eds.), *Diplomacy and the Making of World Politics*, Cambridge 2015, 31–54.
Joseph, J., *The Social in the Global: Social Theory, Governmentality and Global Politics*. Cambridge 2012.
Kiewiet, D. R./McCubbins, M. D., *The Logic of Delegation*, Chicago 1991.
Knutsen, T./Leira, H./Neumann, I. B., *Norsk utenrikspolitikks idehistorie*, 1890–1940, Oslo 2016.
Kolsrud, O., *Rekonstruksjon og reform. Regjeringskontorene 1945-2005*, Oslo 2008.
Krieger, M./Souma, S./Nexon, D., "US military diplomacy in practice", in Sending, O. J., Pouliot, V. and Neumann, I. B. (eds.), *Diplomacy and the Making of World Politics*, 2015, 220–255.
Loder, K., "The Peace Process in Mali", *Security Dialogue*, 28 (1997), 409–24.
Maley, W., "Receiving Afghanistan's Asylum Seekers: Australia, the Tampa 'Crisis' and Refugee Protection", *FMR* 13 (2003), 19–21.

http://www.fmreview.org/en/FMRpdfs/FMR13/fmr13.7.pdf, retrieved 19 January 2015.

Ministry of Foreign Affairs, *Finland, Peace Mediation – Finland's Guidelines*, Helsinki, 2010

Mitchell, T., *Colonising Egypt*, Berkeley, CA 1988.

Mitzen, J., "From Representation to Governing: Diplomacy and the Constitution of International Public Power", in Sending, O. J., Pouliot, V. and Neumann, I. B. (eds.), *Diplomacy and the Making of World Politics*, 2015, 111–139.

Neumann, I. B., "Diplomacy: An Evolutionary Perspective", in Messner, D. and Weinich, S. (eds.), *Global Cooperation and The Human Factor in International Relations*, London 2016, 225–245.

Neumann, I. B., *At Home with the Diplomats: Inside A European Foreign Ministry*, Ithaca, NY 2012.

Neumann, I. B./Sending, O. J., *Governing the Global Polity*, 2010.

Neumann, I. B./Sending, O. J., Ole Jacob Sending (2007) "'The International' as Governmentality", *Millennium*, 35 (2007), 677–701.

Onuf, N., "A Constructivist Manifesto" in Burch, K. and R. Denemark (eds) *Constituting International Political Economy*, Boulder, 1997, 7–20.

Orford, A., *International Authority and the Responsibility to Protect*, Cambridge 2011.

Poggi, G., *The Development of the Modern State: A Sociological Introduction*, London 1978.

Sending, O. J., *The Politics of Expertise: Competing for Authority in Global Governance*, Ann Arbor 2015a.

Sending, O. J., "Diplomats and Humanitarians in Crisis Governance", in Sending, O. J., Pouliot, V. and Neumann, I. B. (eds.), *Diplomacy and the Making of World Politics*, Cambridge 2015b, 256–283.

Vincent, J., Human Rights and International Relations, Cambridge 1986.

Vogt, C. E., *Fridtjof Nansen. Mannen og verden*, Oslo 2011.

Waever, O., "Securitisation and Desecuritisation", in Lipschutz, R. D. (ed.), *On Security*, New York 1995, 46–86.

Wendt, A., "Why a world state is inevitable". *European journal of international relations*, 9 (2003), 491–542.

The Sociology of International Relations in India: Competing Conceptions of Political Order

Siddharth Mallavarapu

The primary intent of this chapter is to present one distinctive non-western scholarly constellation (i.e. Indian) perspectives on how global political order has been theorized and reflected upon in the second half of the twentieth century (i.e. principally during the cold war and the early post-cold war decades). A consistent refrain regarding the discipline of International Relations (IR) is its ethnocentric nature.[1] However, my objective here is to go beyond mere critique and gesture to an alternative inventory of figures and conceptions concerning global order that need to be engaged with and acknowledged within the corpus of global IR scholarship. In the process of enunciating these distinctive voices and positions, I also hope to articulate my own individual perspective with regard to each of these contributions and further to think through how they help forge an overall landscape of political order in some respects that is quite distinctive in texture, tone and sensibility from the Anglo-American mainstream while on occasion also mirroring the global *zeitgeist* at least partially in some clearly discernible fashions. There are two important issues that I shall briefly gesture to in the conclusion—the first relates to the translation of ideas from one locale to another, especially if they entail a degree of contextual exceptionalism and two, how we can further democratize the discipline of IR by introducing into the global episteme, figures and archives from the global south (not merely from Asia but also South America, Africa and the Arab world) that have not received their due at least until now.[2]

More specifically for our purposes here, I focus on seven vignettes of IR scholarship emanating from India playing out across two generations.

---

[1] Acharya and Buzan, Why is There no non-Western International Relations Theory? An Introduction, 287–312.

[2] Mignolo, *Local Histories/Global Designs*. See also Vigneswaran and Quirk, Past Masters and Modern Inventions, 107–131.

My heuristic to access these eclectic worlds is to tease out from these writings issues germane to both the theory and practice of global political order as has been approached by a heterogeneous community of scholars. The key protagonists of these positions include Sisir Gupta, Angadipuram Appadorai, Jayantanuja Bandyopadhyaya and Urmila Phadnis (from the first generation) and Kanti Prasad Bajpai, Bhupinder Singh Chimni and Ashis Nandy (from the second generation). While Gupta and Appadorai were pioneering figures in the Indian variant of the discipline associated with the Indian Council of World Affairs (ICWA) and the Indian School of International Studies (ISIS), which was subsequently rechristened as the School of International Studies (SIS) at Jawaharlal Nehru University (JNU) in New Delhi,[3] Bandyopadhyaya was considered a key figure consolidating the study of IR at the Jadavpur University in Kolkatta. The only other figure from the first generation in this account is Urmila Phadnis who contributed richly to the study of South Asia at the SIS, JNU.

In terms of the second generation, Bajpai re-defined in fundamental ways how theory was taught and viewed from the mid-1990s onwards at the SIS, JNU, while Chimni almost single-handedly (after R.P.Anand from the first generation) built a second generation of Third World Approaches to International Law (TWAIL) scholarship both within India while simultaneously contributing substantively to global thought in this specific domain.[4] A third figure, Nandy never taught International Studies (the precise nomenclature for International Relations) in India. However, he remains well within my remit here because he is a fine mind who has gone out of his way to explicitly address International Relations as a discipline while mincing no words in his often scathing indictment of the discipline's indigenous purveyors of realism as well as of Indian political elites and their uncritical compact with European Enlightenment modernity.[5]

My choice of these figures is not accidental. I have identified some representative voices that speak to the subject of my overarching interest, namely, the latent or explicit theorization of global political order and the insertion of India as a central character in that story. In terms of the first generation, I focus on Appadorai's book length reflection on questions relating to the use of force in international relations, Gupta's thesis on the praxis of regional integration in South Asia, Phadnis on ethno-nationalisms

---

3 Chimni and Mallavarapu, Introduction, xiii–xxiv.
4 See for instance, Anand, *Asian States*.
5 See especially Nandy, The Discreet Charms of Indian Terrorism, 358–391.

and Bandyopadhyaya's evaluation of climate change concerns as a driver of political status quoism in the global North and revisionism in the global South. All these scholarly interventions in my view provide us with a rich palate of both sound empirics and theoretical formulations through which a student of International Relations located anywhere in the world can mull over facets of global political order as viewed from India.

With regard to the second generation, a similar heuristic guides me. I begin with Bajpai who offers us a rich theoretical account of India's standing and strivings in its external realm. He persuasively argues that India may be best understood theoretically through a "modified structural realism" stance. This is followed by an account of Chimni's critical lens that probes India's external engagements in the light of various claims advanced by a unique tradition within International Law referred to as TWAIL. Finally, I treat these contributions not merely as the intellectual property or inheritance of any single civilizational state or disciplinary tradition (in this case that of India's) but indeed of a much wider and compelling global intellectual mural. I have also been keen to showcase some of these interventions in the original language of the relevant authors to give readers a glimpse not merely of their ideas but also most significantly to ensure accuracy and a peek into the stylistics employed to argue their case. I seek your indulgence in this regard.

To reiterate, from a disciplinary point of view, this project remains opens to locating these scholarly contributions not merely in the discursive ecology of the study of International Relations in India but to also see where and how these ideas might cohabit within a wider global conversation around these universal questions. Further, it is perhaps worthwhile to follow up systematically on what implications these interventions might carry for an otherwise conspicuously Anglo-American ethnocentric discipline. There are several recurring themes that surface through a close reading of these myriad contributions. These pertain to both a contending range of political actors (principally the state, but also the role of the major powers of the day and non-state actors) and the concerted advancement on occasion of intertwined claims of both political order and political justice. Without any further disclaimers, I shall now proceed to distilling these seven snapshots of political order as envisaged from an Indian provenance.

Order as Capacity to Negotiate Global Asymmetries: Sisir Gupta and the Quest for a New Indian Grammar of International Relations

Sisir Gupta ranks as arguably the most critical figure in the first generation of Indian International Relations scholarship. By all accounts, he was considered among the brightest of his generation while also serving a stint as a practitioner of diplomacy representing India during his short but illustrious career. He was associated from its early days with the ICWA as also the ISIS subsequently rechristened as the School of International Studies located in Delhi. His best-known book was on Kashmir, but he contributed several other key publications that earned him a wider international reputation. Hedley Bull and Hans Morgenthau (both visiting scholars to the Indian School of International Studies) and other leading lights of the day were aware of his scholarly work and acknowledged his contributions in terms of offering insightful non-western perspectives on Asia and the world.

Gupta wrote an important book in 1964 titled *India and Regional Integration in Asia* which dovetails well with our interest in Indian perspectives on conceptions of global political order. The key issue he contends with is how does India address its search for a better status in a world principally dominated by the major Western powers. Gupta gave thought to a number of key dimensions in the light of this overriding normative interest in regional integration and Asia. These encompassed questions relating to the rise of China in Asia (especially after the Indian debacle with China in 1962), the relevance of a classic doctrine of balance of power, an alternative calendar in terms of what mattered for Asia, the idea of a 'third force' articulated by Nehru, a scrutiny of the Indian opposition to military alliances (which has endured as a continuing refrain in Indian foreign policy) and a prescient summary of the obstacles to regional integration in Asia. These remain prescient considering that regional integration for Asia as a whole still remains an ideal and is not a realized political reality.

Let us step back for a moment in time and sift through some of the key claims advanced in this context. First as relates to regional integration and the growing anticipation of an enlarging Asian footprint of China, Gupta in a postscript to his book was rather categorical. He suggests in this regard that "[w]hat is most relevant for this book, however, is that for the first time the possibility has opened up of a different kind of integration, at least in some parts of Asia" [6]. This is in marked contrast to what

"has been stated earlier that one natural form of integration is when a great power by exercising the sheer weight of its military and economic strength organizes a neighbouring region into some kind of an integrated unit. This type of integration is hardly an immaculate federation and it often becomes difficult to differentiate between this form of integration and the traditional concept of empire-building"[7].

It is in this connection that Gupta expresses his apprehension about China. He notes that "[i]t is of course still a long way for China to tread to become so great and powerful as the Soviet Union or the United States, but there is no doubt that it aspires today to extend its power penumbra over the neighbouring regions and make out parts of Asia and, if possible, Africa an integrated block"[8]. While regional integration could serve some "common stakes" and some "common ends", Gupta is interested in the problematic of how a middle power like India could contain a more powerful and emerging player in the region which is keen on a much larger international presence and status than it then possessed close to the mid-1960s.

Secondly, let us consider the question of the balance of power. What makes Gupta an original thinker is his departure from conventional readings of balance of power in the Indian context. He strays away from any form of simple idealism or malign caricature in his characterization of balance of power and acknowledges that an international system that countenances force with relative balances of power is nothing unusual. Acknowledging G.S.Bajpai (a pioneering Indian practitioner of foreign policy), Gupta quotes him to remind us that

"India is the major stabilizing factor for peace in Asia; the measure of stability that she can impart to this part of the world is not a matter of good intentions but of power [...] It is not power but its misuse or abuse which is morally reprehensible. [...] Thus viewed the ideal of balance of power is nothing evil or incompatible with India's highest ideals."[9]

Gupta argues building on this that "[i]t is the consciousness of the inability of India to play any significant role in the traditional sense of diplomacy

---

6 Gupta, *India and Regional Integration*, 116.
7 Ibid., 116.
8 Ibid., 116.
9 Ibid., 5. See also Bajpai, India and the Balance of Power.

backed by power that governed much of the foreign policy thinking and behavior of the country"[10]. The moral repugnance or stigmatization of power itself as an intrinsic bad is not a line of thinking that he endorses. On the contrary, he is of the considered view that India has to come to terms with the global asymmetries of power and find a way to navigate global order as a relatively weaker state with limited material capabilities. It would need to bring to the fore something new to the table that would give it an independent stature and the accompanying status that it so desires.

The Indian response to the global situation was to introduce a new grammar of 'nonalignment' during the cold war years that "[...] lent Indian policy the distinctive characteristics which have at once made it controversial and complex"[11]. Nehru's response to the cold war may be viewed through the lens of nonalignment. Gupta observes in this connection that "[w]hat is distinctive in this style is the way India has stressed the need to avoid offending any great power. It has often been repeated by Nehru that it was not India's way to shout from the housetops or to use strong language; also, that friendship with one country should not be sought in terms which were hostile to another"[12]. Such a view was not readily accepted particularly by the United States, which remained eternally suspicious of Indian motives during the cold war years. However, in this reading of political order, Gupta reads accurately, that

"the policy of nonalignment was basically an instrument of pursuing the goal of India's national interests; it is therefore, not the negative aspect of this policy of remaining aloof from the cold war alignments but the more positive attempt implicit in this policy of emerging as the area of agreement between the great powers of the world, which should be considered the core of India's foreign policy"[13].

Thirdly, in terms of an alternative almanac for Asia, Gupta gestures to the 1920 Congress of Asian peoples which took place in Baku, the 1927 League Against Imperialism Conference, the 1947 Asian Relations Conference and the 1955 Bandung Conference. All these initiatives must be treated as significant attempts at bringing together the decolonized world and especially Asia together. Gupta argues that Nehru was convinced and therefore went ahead with "[...] the proclamation of Asia's arrival on the

---

10 Ibid., 5.
11 Ibid. 9.
12 Ibid., 26.
13 Ibid., 9.

world scene; the stress on the need for Asian unity; the need to avoid the expression of anti-Western sentiments; and the need for greater regional cooperation"[14].

Fourthly, Gupta evaluates Nehru's idea of the 'third force' as an important corrective to making global influence simply a matter of brute power capabilities. Drawing attention to a 17th February, 1953 speech of Nehru, he observes that Nehru looked at the idea of "a third force" more positively built as it was on ideas of enhancing global cooperation.[15]

Fifthly, an important element of India's strategizing on global political order flowed directly from the doctrine of non-alignment. This involved the eschewal of any form of military alliances. Gupta succinctly captures Indian anxieties as they relate to military alliances. He writes

"[t]he danger of military alliances was that it might shift the focus to other tasks, perpetuate outdated regimes, prevent social reforms, impede economic programmes and thus defeat the very purpose for which they are apparently formed. Moreover, the direct involvement of these countries with the cold war might hinder the all-important need of these countries to underline the issues in world politics which transcended the cold war and communism—the problems created by the growing gap between the developed and underdeveloped countries of the world, the explosive situation created in areas like Africa by racial discrimination and colonial rule, in short, the need for Asians and Africans to be taken into account in world affairs. From these viewpoints, these pacts would reverse the process of history"[16].

Finally, what were some of the key obstacles that Gupta envisaged in terms of a successful regional integration in Asia? He identified twelve such roadblocks. These included geopolitical differences, commonality concerns, disagreements among elites within Asia, the disproportionate influence on some countries (especially China and India), the lack of any single state to force the pace in terms of securing regional integration, the imminent failure of collective security in Asia in the light of their limited capabilities vis-à-vis the West, poor infrastructure to communicate, differing regime types as well as foreign policy orientations, traditional hostilities among some countries in Asia (India-Pakistan, Afghanistan-Pakistan, Philippines-Malaya, Thailand-Cambodia as well as Indonesia-Malaysia), the looming threat of sub-nationalisms and the logic of

---

14 Ibid., 34.
15 Ibid., 49.
16 Ibid., 62.

competition trumping the logic of complementarity. None of these augured well for successful regional integration and thereby Asia had to wait for her moment to challenge the then prevailing global order.[17]

Order as Political Harmony: Angadipuram Appadorai on Great Powers and the Bad Habits of Imperialism

Angadipuram Appadorai was again one of the pioneering figures of the study of International Relations in India. He was a figure who contributed enormously to the institutionalization of International Relations as a discipline in India having played an important role in its early evolution—both at the Indian School of International Studies and subsequently at the School of International Studies.

As far back as 1958, Appadorai authored a book titled *The Use of Force in International Relations*. This intervention serves us as an interesting peg to consider how global political order was viewed by another canonical figure in the first generation of International Relations scholarship in India. The book touches upon several interesting facets relating to our theme under discussion. These include the conceptualization of order as harmony, how order was framed and embedded in the cold war context, the role of ideas and political change, what Gandhi thought about political order and how that might be of relevance to discussing India and the world in the late 1950s. He also addressed himself to how order was inextricably laced with concerns focused on justice evident in his review of some key and yet again prescient global proposals on institutional reform to remedy a persisting "international error of distribution"[18].

According to Appadorai,

"the crux of the problem of harmony in international relations lies in perfecting the means of peaceful change in international society so that there is no temptation on the part of an individual State or of the international community to resort to war, and second, the main function of a universal international organization is to facilitate peaceful change and peaceful settlement of disputes and to lay the social

---

17 Ibid., 102–103.
18 Appadorai, *The Use of Force*, 43.

and economic foundations of peace. The road is hard, but in the revolutionary age in which we are living there is no short cut to peace, security and justice"[19].

Drawing attention to some critical landmarks in history (the 1919 League of Nations Covenant, the 1928 Pact of Paris, and the 1945 Charter of the United Nations), Appadorai questioned the implications of the collective security doctrine and its application in a nuclear age marked by ideological confrontation. Ideas mattered in history, but he argued that quite evidently history demonstrates that not all ideas succeed. The ones that succeed require both astute leadership and statecraft as also most significantly the support of the people. In the absence of any of these criteria, ideas are not likely to succeed.

Invoking Gandhi, Appadorai also delves into issues of great power socialization and asks whether they will be able to stray away from more imperialist modes of domination. He quotes Gandhi in this regard as stating unambiguously the following truism:

"It is open to the great powers to take up non-violence any day and cover themselves with glory and earn the eternal gratitude of posterity. If they or any of them can shed the fear of destruction, if they disarm themselves, they will automatically help the rest to regain their sanity. But then these great powers have to give up imperialistic ambitions and exploitation of the so-called uncivilized or semi-civilized nations of the earth and revise their mode of life. It means a complete revolution. Great nations can hardly be expected in the ordinary course to move spontaneously in the direction of the one they followed, and, according to their notion of value, from victory to victory. But miracles have happened before and may happen even in this prosaic age"[20].

At one plane, this might seem as fairly elementary and wishful thinking but it still makes the normative case for change in a definite direction as positive and possible. However, this would hinge on structural transformations reflected in our collective behaviour as well as the willingness of the arbiters of power to let go of the habits of imperialism. A tall order indeed but given the only other option of "impending doom", we may be compelled as Appadorai suggests to come to concede "[…] the nonviolent method with all its glorious implications"[21].

---

19 Ibid., 38.
20 Ibid., 36–37.
21 Ibid., 37.

Two global proposals for institutional reform that attract the attention of Appadorai during this period are those posited by G.Clark and L.B.Sohn and that of Lord Davies. In the case of the former,

"[t]he gist of their proposals is disarmament through law: competitive armaments is the villain of the piece in world anarchy today and the only solution is universal disarmament, complete and enforceable through a rigid system of inspection, only strictly limited and lightly armed forces being permitted to nation-states for internal order only. The revised United Nations will therefore be a federation of all nations to enforce compulsory national disarmament and fully equipped to prevent or promptly suppress any wars between *any* nations. The powers of the Federation would be restricted to matters *directly* related to the prevention of war, though within this field they would also be adequate; but outside the field, it should have no authority whatever to recommend"[22].

With regard to the latter proposal extended by Lord Davies, Appadorai argues that that "his thoughtful book *The Problem of the Twentieth Century* is worth careful exploration, viz., the principle of differentiation"[23]. Appadorai observes that

"[s]tarting from the idea that the international authority should have an international force under its control and direction with which to keep the peace, Lord Davies developed the idea that the most powerful weapons which had come into existence in the course of the war (the First World War) were to be allotted to the international force. All research and development of new weapons were to be under the control of the international authority so that its preponderance could never be challenged"[24].

A final but critical area of reform suggested when it comes to re-conceptualizing political order in Appadorai's frame was the reform of the United Nations. What he had to convey in the 1950s still remains an unrealized goal. He argued that

"[t]he Security Council's membership may be raised to fifteen. The veto will continue to be vested in the five permanent members which already have it; and to give additional protection to the powers without veto the concurring votes of a majority of them should be required for enforcement action, although the General Assembly may be permitted to recommend the voluntary use of force and to co-

---

22 Ibid., 94.
23 Ibid., 96.
24 Ibid., 96.

ordinate such use by members of the United Nations in case of a State engaged in hostility refuses to accept cease-fire"[25].

Appadorai like many of his generation vested hope in a rehabilitated United Nations that would carry out reforms and argued that ultimately "[...] the ideal solution is to convert the United Nations into a federal State with the one limited function of prevention of war and the maintenance of peace"[26]. However, he also recognized that absent a pending change in classical modes of Westphalian sovereignty there remained little chance of any such fundamental metamorphosis.

The Case for a New International Climate Order: Jayantanuja Bandhyopadhyaya on Averting the Fate of the New International Economic Order

A unique vantage point to examine theorizations of global political order is best exemplified in the work of Jayantanuja Bandyopadhyaya. His work on the need to recalibrate a global climate order consciously raises first order questions relating to culpability and distributive inequity issues that straddle the schisms of the global North and the global South. Bandyopadhyaya places an emphasis on the burden of history and how imperialism has morphed into neo-imperialism in the current international order.

He observes in this context that

"[a]n understanding of the present structure of international relations, or of the essential conditions for the establishment of a future world order, would be impossible unless the climatic factor as a global resource is brought into the picture. It is necessary to understand the global distribution of the macroclimate, the broad effects of the major climatic types on the economic, political and cultural development of a region, and the manner in which these regional climatic impacts affect the capabilities and relations of nations. Any futuristic design of world order, should also pay attention to the redistribution of the global macroclimate, as of other global resources"[27].

However, critical to this narrative is the underlying assertion that

---

25 Ibid., 105–106.
26 Ibid., 106.
27 Bandyopadhyaya, *Climate and World Order*, 6.

"[c]limate is thus at least one of the major factors which may explain the origin and the continuance of the North-South dichotomy. While imperialism is undoubtedly the greatest single *historical* force responsible for the North-South economic gap, climate is perhaps the greatest single *natural* factor in the origin and development of the gap"[28].

One of the principal challenges then remains "[...] the elimination of this dichotomy [a]s one of the prerequisites to the establishment of a stable and viable world order"[29].

There remain in Bandyopadhyaya's assessment deeper biases in the manner in which questions around climate change are framed. He is of the view that the tropical climate of the global South impacts economic productivity while the temperate climate of the global North is favourable to greater economic productivity. While pointing a finger towards the North in terms of culpability for particularly excessive levels of global consumption, he is critical of scholarship in the South that overlooks these clear distinctions. He argues that

"the literature of the North is delightfully vague, when not altogether silent, on the possible repercussions in the South of the climatic changes in the North. In their usually ethnocentric way, the scholars of the North presume that climatic change in the North would call the tune, and climatic change in the South would respond to it in some vague, undefined, indeterminate and groping manner"[30].

While the North here is seen as pushing for climate change status quoism, it is the South which is revisionist in this domain. The North's status quoism translates into an accent "[...] on the study of climatic variability, climatic monitoring, climatic modeling, climatic impact, and preparation of alternative strategies for maintaining the climatic status quo. All available scholars, organizations and institutions in the North, particularly in the Northwest, have been mobilized for their purpose"[31]. In marked contrast, Bandyopadhyaya argues that

"just as in case of the New International Economic Order it is necessary for countries of the South to mobilize their manpower and natural resources for accelerated national economic development, side by side with a global struggle against the North, so also it is necessary for them to make certain changes in their national cultures for minimizing the adverse impacts of the tropical macroclimate,

---

28 Ibid., 4.
29 Ibid., 4.
30 Ibid., 104.
31 Ibid., 106.

along with a struggle for global climatic amelioration. This cultural adaptation to climate world would consist essentially of a direct transition of the South to a cybernetic society, without passing through the so-called stages of economic growth experienced by the industrially developed countries of the North"[32].

Thus Bandyopadhyaya introduces the idea of leap-frogging and also rejects Schumacher's *Small is Beautiful* logic. He remains convinced "[...] that if Schumacher's programme is accepted in the Third World, it would not only lead to a further widening of the techno-economic gap between the North and the South, but also to the perpetuation of the neo-imperialistic stranglehold of the former over the latter"[33].

The overall drift of Bandyopadhyaya's account is to treat global political order as an effort by the powerful states to impose their writ on weaker and unsuspecting players in the international system. He may have articulated an early claim from within International Relations on the idea of 'climate justice' that also is succinctly captured in the slogan 'common but differentiated responsibilities' which has become the mainstay of much of the developing world's standpoint on climate change issues. The other category which provides an overall theoretical vantage point for Bandyopadhyaya is neo-imperialism, where he argues that historical inequities have resulted in a world which is not a *tabula rasa* but is weighed against former colonies and contemporary postcolonial states. It is important for these states to be particularly wary of any further efforts at encroachment of their sovereign space by the erstwhile colonial powers and any new claimants to the project of Empire. Climate change remains one register in which vigilance in the global South is warranted but this would also extend for instance to newer doctrines of humanitarian intervention and regime change. The promise of the New International Economic Order remained unrealized and this time around climate change could provide an important site to reconfigure and rehabilitate relations between the global North and the global South on a more equitable basis.

---

32 Ibid., 137.
33 Ibid., 142.

Ethnicity, Nation-Building and the Global Political Order: Urmila Phadnis on South Asian Perspectives

An interesting departure in terms of thinking theoretically about global political order is exemplified in the work of one of India's eminent South Asianists, Urmila Phadnis. As a professor at the School of International Studies, she lent intellectual stewardship to an entire generation of South Asian studies and contributed a seminal volume on *Ethnicity and Nation-Building in South Asia*. While the book focuses specifically on the regional dimensions of ethnicity in South Asia, it also scrutinizes the role of external actors and how ethno-nationalisms come to be narrowly construed as a consequence of specific historical experiences. Her principal hypothesis is that

"ethnic identity is significant but not a sufficient requisite for evoking ethnicity. It is the mobilization and manipulation of a group identity and interest by the leadership that leads to ethnicity. Ethnicity is harnessed as an ideology as well as a device to wrest greater concessions and share in the institution of power and authority"[34].

From our perspective here, what makes Phadnis's intervention relevant is her evaluation of European inheritances in terms of modern nation-statehood in South Asia and the ensuing discomfiture and perceptions of 'vulnerability' among state elites. Distinguishing between an 'ethnicist' and 'statist' perspective with regard to approaching questions of political community, she is keen on introducing nuance in how South Asia figures in the broader global narrative within this context. Phadnis perceptively observes in this regard that

"[e]nsconced in the historical experiences of the western world, the dominant premise of both the perspectives has been able to relate the evolution of nation-states with the process of industrial revolution and the rise of capitalism. Hence the 'modernness' of the concept. However, some of the recent writings reflect a greater degree of sensitivity to the complexities of its socio-cultural bases. Thus, while nation-states are considered to be 'new', it is emphasized that the 'nations' to which they give political expression loom out of an immemorial past"[35].

Thus, the idea of civilizational states as a distinct category of states enters this picture.

---

34 Phadnis, *Ethnicity and Nation-Building*, 8.
35 Ibid., 23–24.

Phadnis also extends her critique to the manner in which international organizations have been characterized. She writes

"[a]s regards the statist approach, the European heritage of the term nation-state has pervaded global terminology as is evident from nomenclature like the League of Nations, the United Nations, International Politics, the International Court of Justice. Strictly speaking, these are misnomers but the very usage of the term reflects the mood and orientations of the people who mattered, regarding these terms"[36].

Further, the complications of regime type in South Asia warrant a certain degree of attention to how political change is approached. When it comes to India, Phadnis notes that

"any discussion on the Indian state in the South Asian context must reckon with one pertinent fact: the levels of politics needs to be taken note of as much as the language of politics. In the Indian context, thus, as the discussion has *a priori*, a democratic framework as its referent, focus has to be on the structures and processes sustaining, strengthening or subverting or weakening it. That need not be the frame of reference for a military regime in the context of which the discussion hinges on the resurrection or restoration of a democratic and participatory mechanism with issues of credibility, legitimacy, and accountability closely related therein"[37].

There has also been a tendency to over-centralization in South Asia given the specific trajectories of post-colonial statehood. She observes that

"[a]s regards the state, its increasing role has been bequeathed by colonialism and reinforced by the espousal of development, equity and justice by the post-colonial leadership. Besides, a strong Centre was necessitated to cope with issues of identity and territoriality. Thus, the respective 'territorial centre' of these states became pivotal for state activities"[38].

Ethno nationalism remains a peculiar species of nationalism. Phadnis argues that

"[t]he broad contours of the state system in South Asian countries reflects the pull and diversity in socio-economic and political terms as well as the push of the central leadership to reconcile the substance of diversity in the concept of the

---

36 Ibid., 21.
37 Ibid., 66.
38 Ibid., 81.

'nation'. In most cases the leadership has found it difficult to come to terms on this issue as is evident from ethnic politics in South Asia"[39].

One facet which receives special attention in Phadnis's account is the role of external powers in fomenting ethnic claims of one kind or the other in South Asia. The contingent configurations of power and the balance of power also impacts how domestic outcomes unfold in the context of these claims. Phadnis argues that

"[t]he nature and extent of such support has hinged on the calculations of its costs and benefits at the official and unofficial levels in various states. At the government level, factors that have influenced such calculations have been systemic, strategic and ideological within the wider gamut of the state's foreign policy objectives and goals"[40].

The slants of emphasis in Phadnis's work also squarely confront the palpable tensions between the theory and practice of state sovereignty as a generic principle in international affairs. She observes that

"[i]n the contemporary international system, the inviolability of an existing state is a universally recognized value. Following from this, separatism is viewed by the states as an anathema, which should not be endorsed as it threatens the sovereignty and territorial integrity of a state. Such a *status quoist* stance gets further buttressed in view of the fact that most countries are multi-ethnic states"[41].

However, she goes on to suggest that

"[s]uch a view is normative. In practice, however, the separatist movements in South Asia and elsewhere have found in external support an important source of sustenance. While moral support has been provided in the form of internationalization of the seperatists' grievances by emphasizing the aspects of human rights, discrimination and oppression of the ethnic group, material support has taken the form of operation bases, military training, military equipment, economic aid, etc."[42].

Ultimately, Phadnis also draws attention to the issue of resource paucity and the potential for conflict in such situations. She claims that

"the challenges of ethnicity and nation-building, operating in a highly complex nexus of society, economy and polity, hinge on the issues of access and stakes in the power structure. In this context, the experiences of the South Asian states are

---

39 Ibid., 82.
40 Ibid., 239.
41 Ibid., 238.
42 Ibid., 238–239.

instructive as well as illuminating. These polyethnic societies are characterized by greater ethnic diversity than perhaps any other region in the world. However, in terms of boundary delineation, levels of development, content, context, constraints, as well as the potential of the varied demands for recognition, power and status, uniformities as well as variations among the ethnic groups across the borders can be discerned"[43].

Thus, Phadnis offers us a compelling and coherent narrative that provides us yet another lens to think about global political order. The strong emphasis placed on contingency, location and the influence of history on modern state formation in South Asia makes for a specific reading of the international situation and recognition of key constraints as well as opportunities that the contingent opens up. In effect, this is a grim reminder of the tensions between idea and reality, percept and practice in international politics both at the national and international levels of analysis.

Disparate Indian Traditions of Political Order: Typologist *Par Excellence*, Kanti Bajpai

The most comprehensive and definitive effort till date from within the discipline of International Relations to rigorously approach Indian traditions of thinking through questions of political order may be found in the scholarly work of Kanti Bajpai. In a contribution which appeared in 2003 titled 'Indian Conceptions of Order and Justice: Nehruvian, Gandhian, Hindutva and Neo-Liberal', Bajpai crisply interrogates four distinct modes of approaching political order from within the Indian setting. These include the 'Nehruvian', 'Gandhian', the 'Hindutva' and 'Neo-Liberal' conceptions.[44] Each of these traditions of thinking about order makes a very clear set of arguments about what matters in this context and how India might best respond to these images under the current global circumstances.

The first and perhaps longest enduring tradition of thinking about political order in post-independence India emerges from the *weltanschaung* of its first Prime Minister, Jawaharlal Nehru. In Bajpai's reading of

---

43 Ibid., 29.
44 Bajpai, Indian Conceptions of Order and Justice, 236–261.

Nehruvianism, he acknowledges some distinctive traits. These include a certain willingness to reckon with political realism, a suspicion about the stability of balance of power arrangements, a recognition that states might sometimes take recourse to force which remains both unavoidable and on occasion desirable though never a guarantor of peace, the vitality of nonalignment and a willingness to contend with ideas like world government and world federation which potentially were ahead of their time but might find realization with the creation of appropriate conditions to make them a reality.[45]

What is Bajpai's verdict on Nehru? He argues,

"[i]n the end, Nehruvians have had little choice but to accept post-war rules and institutions. This is clear from India's policies on the role of the great powers in the United Nations (UN) and on global economic redistribution. While nonalignment signified that much of the world rejected the idea of an exceptional role for the great powers, India, as an original participant in the setting up of the UN, and in pursuit of international order, had in fact accepted great power exceptionalism in terms of the veto of the Permanent Five. Nehruvian India ultimately has always made the point that the world body should eventually be made more equitable and accountable. Similarly, the Nehruvian demand for international collaboration in regulating the global economy and reducing economic inequality was made within the constraints of a Westphalian order"[46].

The second distinct conception of political order, which Bajpai discusses at some length draws from Mahatma Gandhi. According to this perspective, the individual is the ultimate locus of ethical conduct. It places a strong emphasis on individual agency, privileges local knowledge, advances the case for both political and economic decentralization, privileges justice over order and regards non-violence as political credo combined with a quest for equity and truth. According to this image, "[o]rder will result from the interactions within and between small, economically self-sufficient, face-to-face communities—the real, acting unit of world politics. The key characteristics of those interactions must be ahimsa (non-violence), satyagraha ('truth power'), and economic equity"[47].

Gandhi departs from Marx, not so much in terms of the diagnosis of global inequity but in his rejection of violence as a means to recalibrate class injustices. There is a much stronger belief in the role of "[p]ersuasion

---

45 Ibid., 243–244.
46 Ibid.
47 Ibid., 245.

and self-regulation, more than coercion" when it comes to "build[ing] a lasting and just order"[48].

What is Bajpai's overall verdict when it comes to Gandhi's contribution to thinking about political order? According to him,

"[i]n sum, the Gandhian challenge to Westphalia is to replace an international order built on states and the regulated use of violence with a world order compromising relations among individuals, groups, communities and states based on non-violence and economic equality. The rights and responsibilities of collectivities—groups, communities, states, and the world as a whole. In [Hedley] Bull's terms, Gandhians can be said to favour the claims of individual and cosmopolitan justice over international order"[49].

A third and another distinctive outlook on political order emerges from the Hindu right in India. In Bajpai's assessment, the underlying premises of this perspective stem from its accent on cultural nationalism, a strong endorsal of state sovereignty, the explication of civilizational virtues, the recognition of great power influence on the constitution of rules, the brute reality of hierarchy and viewed in its benign incarnations as more desirable than 'strict equality', the reliance on both soft and hard power and the ultimate goal of realizing a 'Hinduized order'.[50]

According to Bajpai,

"[a]t one level, the Hindutva view of order is compatible with traditional Westphalia. Its proponents do not reject the basic rules and institutions of Westphalian order, including the notion of state sovereignty. The Hindutva view accepts the importance of institutions such as the balance of power and the exceptionalism of great powers. With time, when Indians rehabilitate themselves and acknowledge their essential Hindu identity, India will be in a position to join the great power oligarchy at the top of the international order. India's claims will be based not simply on its power but also on its civilizational greatness and cultural contributions to the world. Hindutva proponents offer little commentary on international law and organization, although, like the Nehruvians and Gandhians, they fear that the rules and institutions of international society may be captive to great-power interests"[51].

A third conception of political order remains distinctively neoliberal in flavor. In this idiom, both states and markets matter, however, states must

---

48 Ibid., 247.
49 Ibid., 248.
50 Ibid., 252.
51 Ibid., 249.

play a role in ensuring the smooth functioning of markets. Further, India would stand to gain by partnering with the West, there is always the likelihood of classical geopolitics trumping Western 'norms and procedures' and the ever present possibility of the West not meeting the standards it espouses.[52]

Bajpai suggests that the neoliberal conception is not incompatible with traditional Westphalia. Neoliberals are also willing to acknowledge a central role for states. However, the buck does not stop here. Bajpai argues that for neoliberals

"[t]he interdependence of major-power war should, in this interdependent world, gradually decline because the powerful states will be in the forefront of globalization. International law and organizations will play a role not so much in regulating war as in ensuring that a worldwide system of economic exchange is established and protected. Regionalism and multilateralism in economic affairs will increase. War will decline, but global violence may well increase as some non-state actors resist in this globalizing world economy and as parochial forces, such as ethnic and religious extremists resort to violence. States therefore will also increasingly be focused on how to deal with non-state actors"[53].

Another seminal intervention of Bajpai with regard to India's ambitions and pursuits in the domain of state security are also relevant to our interest in how political order has come to be viewed in India. Drawing on Stephen Krasner's notion of modified structuralism,[54] Bajpai extends this conceptual repertoire to contemporary India. He claims in this connection that

"[t]wo interpretations of India's modified structural realism can be advanced. In the first interpretation, modified structuralism arises from expediency. Given the magnitude of the external threats facing India and its internal vulnerabilities—in the areas of military strength, economic development and internal order—the country must combine coercive with accommodative strategies as a way of compensating for its weaknesses"[55].

This is in contrast to 'second interpretation' where

"modified structuralism is a function of conviction. Power is India's ambition; but Indian decision makers understand that power-seeking provokes power-seeking, force begets force. Beyond a certain point, then, power approaches are self-

---

52 Ibid., 259.
53 Ibid., 255.
54 Krasner, Structural Causes and Regime Consequences, 185–205.
55 Bajpai, India: Modified Structuralism, 194.

defeating; they may provoke the very outcome that it seeks to avoid, even if it is visited on an adversary is unacceptable. The pursuit of power without supplementary strategies designed to accommodate others or to change attitudes could end in physical or moral disaster. The urge to power must therefore be moderated"[56].

The final verdict in this reading is that "[...] India will remain a modified structuralist state—for the sake of conviction rather than expediency—to the benefit of international peace and stability in the twenty-first century"[57].

'Just World Order(s)': B. S. Chimni on Sri Aurobindo and the Global State

Another distinctive illustration of a second generation of imaginative International Relations scholarship in India is exemplified in the contributions of B. S. Chimni. He has given considerable thought to questions of political order and has also mined indigenous resources to advance eclectic conceptions focused on these questions from an Indian provenance.

Re-reading the contributions of a well-known Indian anti-colonial nationalist Sri Aurobindo, Chimni argues that Aurobindo in his book *The Ideal of Human Unity* expressed his

"preference [...] for a loose confederation of humankind that preserved the diversity of peoples and nations as against a centralized world state that would encourage human uniformity. From this standpoint, Sri Aurobindo saw the League of Nations and United Nations as welcome steps in the direction of the emergence of a democratic world state, albeit as he was critical of both from the viewpoint of egalitarian politics and the absence in the international community of any understanding of the need for spiritual human unity to accompany what he termed 'mechanical unity'."[58]

Distinguishing Marx from Aurobindo, Chimni observes that

---

56 Ibid., 195.
57 Ibid., 197.
58 Chimni, Retrieving 'Other' Visions, 132.

"unlike Marx, he did not articulate an elaborate theory of social change. He increasingly came to focus more on the spiritual quest of the individual than on collective social struggle to bring about social transformation. I argue instead that the inner transformation that Sri Aurobindo stresses can inter alia be brought about through participating in ethical collective struggles for a just world order"[59].

Chimni also warns against erecting any simplistic Oriental binary to decipher Aurobindo's oeuvre. He argues that

"[i]t is important to emphasize, however, that Sri Aurobindo did not dismiss material progress, and his way of thinking therefore does not fit the neat stereotype of the materialist West and the spiritual East. Indeed, he offers a unique understanding that allows a simultaneous commitment to reason, ethical politics, and individual spiritual growth"[60].

In his 2005 article on 'Alternative Visions of Just World Order', Chimni distinguishes between six perspectives on 'just world order'. These include what he refers to as the 'establishment perspective', the 'left', 'dalit', 'subaltern', 'anti-modernist' and the 'spiritual' perspective (read Sri Aurobindo) all of which offer us diverse representations of how both justice and political order could be theorized.[61] While the 'establishment perspective' is best represented here through well-known works like *In Defence of Globalization* by Jagdish Bhagwati, the other perspectives merit further elaboration here. Chimni's own work very much belongs to the Left tradition and also finds articulation in his contributions to the TWAIL body of scholarship. According to Chimni,

"[t]he Left identifies the rise of international financial capital as the major social force with the potential to subvert dependent and dominant economies. This development has led to the loss of economic sovereignty and the institutionalization of polyarchy in Third World states. In their view, democracy has been reduced to a choice between different political parties with essentially the same economic program, and any attempt to resist domination invites the hostility of the imperial world led by the United States"[62].

The Dalit perspective in Chimni's reading treats globalization as a positive development given that it weakens traditional identities that have often been to the detriment of particular communities at the receiving end of

---

59 Ibid., 132.
60 Chimni, Alternative Visions of Just World Orders, 398–399.
61 Ibid., 389–402.
62 Ibid., 392.

history. Globalization also heightens international awareness of the plight of those located at the margins of both national and international society. The Subaltern perspective when applied to the study of international law through the work of scholars like Dianne Otto, Chimni points out also draws attention to claims around the New International Economic Order. Ashis Nandy surfaces in this narrative as an exponent of the 'anti-modernist' stance skeptical as he is of Enlightenment rationality, development with a big D and history with a big H, doctrines belying the promises they hold out.[63]

In more recent years, Chimni has also written at some length about the idea of a 'global state' but thinking through the politics of what a 'global welfare state' might look like. He notes in this regard that "[t]he emergence of a Global State has meant *a global class divide is overlaying the North-South divide creating a complex map of global fractures*"[64]. Chimni goes on to add that "[w]hile the emerging non-territorial Global State [...] is imperial in character, it can be transformed into a Global Welfare State if only the international community can adhere to basic principles and practices that [...] constitute the idea of global justice [...]"[65].

This slice of scholarship also draws renewed attention to the diverse registers in which political order has been viewed in the Indian context. Justice in this rendition is also inseparable from considerations of political order. The drivers of change are not purely material but also involve ideational and inner transformation of individuals as possibilities for more enduring change. Political order today continues to service the interests of global capital and it is oftentimes difficult according to Chimni to distinguish between how political elites speak in different countries because they appear to have bought into the same logic with minor shades of difference. On balance, Chimni places his hope on waging collective struggles that are not confined to any one particular location. They will often need to build global constituencies of like-minded people interested in probing the limits of contemporary global capitalism and bearing in mind that the global North and the global South are real entities and not categories that are denuded of any real content.

---

63 Ibid., 393–395.
64 Chimni, A Just World under Law, 201.
65 Ibid., 203.

Global Political Order as *'The Intimate Enemy'*: Ashis Nandy's Heuristic

Ashis Nandy is a cultural theorist and social psychologist who over his long and distinguished career has offered a whole range of interesting insights into the workings of the Indian psyche and the implications these findings hold when it comes to interpreting politics. His best known work is titled *The Intimate Enemy* where he delves into the life worlds of the colonizer and the colonized and the inescapable impact each has on the other as a consequence of the colonial encounter. He is the author of several other critical commentaries and I merely sample some of his ideas here to tease out the implications it might carry for thinking about yet another Indian perspective on global political order.[66]

Nandy has been rather critical of modernity in its European Enlightenment version particularly in the manner in which it sought to impose its writ in the formerly colonized and now postcolonial world. He argues in this connection that

"man-made suffering is a joint product of the life-styles, systems of knowledge and theories of liberation populating the world stage and after about two centuries of hegemony, the culture of modern Europe and North America no longer arouses the enthusiasm which, as a critique of traditions, it once aroused in the Third World. The first generation of social reformers in colonized societies hoped to use modernity as a vector within the Asian and African traditions, something which would by providing an outsider's critique, help them recover certain recessive aspects of these traditions to give more strength and vivacity to the traditions. It is now fairly obvious that such controlled use of modernity has not been possible in the savage world. Modernity is not only triumphant in the southern hemisphere; it has taken over as an imperial principle in human consciousness in society after society. What was dissent has now become civilization".[67]

Nandy in an interesting reconstruction of a hijacking episode in a piece titled 'The Discreet Charms of Indian Terrorism' also speaks of the need to depart from hackneyed and simplistic realist caricatures of these episodes and instead delve into the 'vernacular' and unacknowledged sensibilities that are present in the wider civil society in the region and elsewhere in the postcolonial world.[68] One recurring theme in Nandy's

---

66 See also Mallavarapu, States, Nationalisms and Modernities in Conversation, 39–70.
67 Nandy, Shamans, Savages and the Wilderness, 270.
68 Nandy, The Discreet Charms of Indian Terrorism, 358–391.

writings deals with civilizational futures. In his piece titled, 'Shamans, Savages and Wilderness: On the Audibility of Dissent and the Future of Civilizations', he argues that "[t]he recovery of the other selves of cultures and communities, selves not defined by the dominant consciousness, may turn out to be the first task of social criticism and political activism and the first responsibility of intellectual stock-taking in the first decade of the coming century." He persuasively contends that "[...] before envisioning the global civilization of the future, one must first own up the responsibility of creating a space at the margins of the present global civilization for a new plural, political ecology of knowledge"[69].

Nandy is hopeful that the Third World despite its many weaknesses also throws up solutions to the global problems of the day. He observes that '[t]he third world is often a target of supervision and patronage, but it can be made a symbol of planetary intellectual responsibility, even despite the Third World. The experience of the Third World can be turned into something more than the record of its individual nation-states. It can be read as a text on survival which hides a code of transcendence"[70].

While it would be a futile exercise to reduce Nandy's complex oeuvre to any simple formulation, there is much here that has a bearing on how questions relating to global political order can itself be approached. He offers us a distinctive heuristic that addresses the legacies of European Enlightenment modernity, the hubris and appetite of capitalism and the violence that it has generated and most importantly a cautionary note against the steamrolling of eclectic knowledge systems into standardized straightjackets to comprehend the many worlds we inhabit.[71] Nandy is keen to widen our repertoire of available epistemological gambits to access the contemporary international system and also delve into intellectual histories of figures from forgotten countries and contexts to revitalize our sense of how best we could re-invent our notion of selves and communities which brings us much closer to an ecologically equitable and much more just world order.

---

[69] Nandy, Shamans, Savages and the Wilderness, 266–267.
[70] Ibid., 275.
[71] Nandy, *Traditions, Tyranny, and Utopias*.

Conclusion

Where have we arrived through these seven distinctive accounts? I want to focus on two facets here. First, what are the specific takeaways from the Indian experience of political thought (chronicled here) with regard to thinking about political order? Second, how can we meaningfully incorporate some of these findings within the global corpus of IR? In other words, what does the act of translation entail here and further how IR epistemologies and ontologies can be further democratized.

Each of the seven thinkers chronicled here came up with different responses to questions of political order. To Gupta, political order was best reflected in the manner in which the newly decolonized Indian state some decades into its existence as an independent nation-state negotiated global asymmetries. He concedes the value of a sturdy realism, predicts the rise of China, argues the relevance of balance of power, treats nonalignment as a significant contribution, reassesses the Nehruvian idea of the 'third force' and draws attention to India's traditional suspicion of military alliances while also examining potential challenges to Asian integration.

Appadorai's conceives of political order as 'harmony' and makes evident his normative anchorage in the idea of 'peaceful change'. The challenge for the great powers as far in this account is to depart from the old bad habit of imperial domination. Order to Appadorai was also ultimately incumbent on the legitimacy of the international system. This would depend on how well inequities reflected in exiting international institutional arrangements, such as for instance the pending reform of the United Nations Security Council (UNSC) would eventually be addressed.

To Bandyopadhyaya, a 'viable world order' would require us to overcome the North-South binary. While imperialism was perceived as kicking and alive, climate change politics was yet another site where traditional geopolitical concerns continued to dominate. In his account, the North comes across as 'status quoist' in terms of retention of privileges and the South as 'revisionist', a claim to revise and ultimately dismantle contemporary structures of privilege. While climate change could provide one potential site for the recalibration of North-South equations, order to Bandyopadhyaya in this realm as well will have to contend with lending content to ideas of 'climate justice'.

Phadnis's conception of political order builds on a suspicion of the role of external powers in fomenting conflicts in the decolonized world. For order to be stable and durable, these impulses have to be forestalled and the contradictions surrounding international state sovereignty as a principle and its actual operationalization need to be redressed.

In terms of the second generation, Bajpai makes an eloquent case for diverse conceptions of global political order residing within the Indian political space—these include the 'Nehruvian', 'Gandhian', 'Hindutva' and 'Neo-Liberal' strains. We learn from this account that Nehruvians were compelled to come to terms with an inequitable international system with its own rules of the game, Gandhians rejected the logic of big capitalism and associated lifestyles as a panacea for newly decolonized states setting out. Non-violence was the building block of a new political order especially if it had to be durable. A third contender in terms of framing political order is Hindutva. This is premised on cultural nationalism as providing the rationale for a much greater footprint in politics of older civilizational states like India and finally the Neo-liberal account places a stronger accent on mutual interdependence and the salience of assorted non-state actors in also determining both political processes and outcomes.

Chimni's reliance on Sri Aurobindo leads us to another conception of political order that is not based purely on 'mechanical unity' but also advances a conception of 'spiritual human unity'. Ultimately, an egalitarian international order will have to serve as the basis of the setting up of a 'democratic world state'. Besides this, Chimni also presents us with six distinctive Indian positions on just world order, which spread across the entire political continuum.

Finally, Nandy mounts an attack on European Enlightenment Modernity with a big 'M'. He contrasts the dystopias these processes have generated in marked contrast to the utopias they promised. More significantly, IR and its traditional version of realism does considerable damage to the political imagination even in the postcolony with state elites replicating the logics of the Westphalian state. He makes a persuasive case for rethinking both the epistemologies and ontologies of post-coloniality afresh as part of a project of resisting the legacies of Eurocentrism.

There are seven key claims that I would like to advance at the end of our journey chronicling two generations of representative Indian International Relations assessments of global political order. First, there is considerable eclecticism in the manner in which order has been theorized within the fold of Indian International Relations thinking. There are several approaches and contending schools of thought evident. For any student of Indian political order, it would be a useful exercise to ask which of these strands have been ascendant at different moments in India's history. It would be misplaced to attribute or impose any single essentialist or monolithic view of political order emanating from India.

Secondly, the distinct slants of emphases reveal distinct political, epistemological and ontological preferences. However, none of these readings are entirely autonomous. In reality, notwithstanding sometimes rather distinctive claims, these perspectives have often been in conversation with each other either by endorsement or by way of critique. They have often surfaced in response to specific moments in national and international political developments.

Thirdly, normative considerations in dealing with political order have been omnipresent. None of these conceptions have been cast as independent of a moral universe. They have often complained about double standards and disillusionment with the actual translation of some of these ideas into practice but they have not ceased to articulate their preference for a particular normative framing of the issues under consideration. Fourthly, order is never viewed as an exclusive category. It inevitably stumbles onto questions of political justice. It may be argued that it is virtually impossible to have a conversation about political order without simultaneously invoking and contesting alternative models of political justice.

Fifthly, quite clearly competing sensibilities determine the nature of the conversation about political order. This flows from distinctive normative preferences that are often explicitly articulated when it comes to discussions around political order.

Sixthly, there is an evident tension in many of these readings between the conceptualization of political order and its actual operationalization. Finally, while order appears to be a generic and universal concern across diverse civilizational frames and political communities, there still is a case to be made for specific political exceptionalisms while thinking about order in particular contexts.

It is perhaps fair to ask what this thought experiment portends for International Relations as a discipline more generically especially in terms of translation and global incorporation of these sensibilities. It is important to emphasize that a fairly large and sophisticated body of thinking has arguably always existed with regard to questions such as global political order within non-western scholarly constellations. India merely served as one illustration here. It would be no surprise to find at least some Wittgensteinian 'family resemblances' in the eclecticism and sophistication of thought within Africa, South America, the Arab world and other Asian settings as well. Similar comparative mapping exercises may throw up an array of thinkers, archives and heuristic possibilities while thinking about political order. Many of these ideas as they deal with broad historical developments within the wider international system have a resonance that extends well beyond national discursive boundaries. The discipline might stand to gain if it listens to these voices more carefully in the years to come. Alternatively, if the discipline is complacent about its reliance on merely one or two mainstream traditions of thinking about political order, it might leave us with a rather impoverished account of this otherwise rich domain of both political thought and action.

A number of concerns have recurred through these accounts. For any interested researcher there are a host of enticing questions and research puzzles worth pondering over in this connection. To begin with we could ask how sovereignty has been viewed across time. Second, is sovereignty assigned a greater sanctity in postcolonial climes as opposed to Westphalia? Third, if order and justice are so deeply intertwined does it make any methodological sense to study them distinctively anymore? Ultimately, we may wish to ask what concepts are germane to the Indian milieu. These are concerns worth pondering over further before articulating the contours of a different vocabulary and grammar of IR building ultimately premised on different experiential realities and allied perceptions anchored in much more varied political imaginaries.

References

Acharya, A./Buzan, B, "Why is there no non-Western international relations theory? An introduction", *International Relations of the Asia-Pacific*, 7:3 (2007), 287–312.
Anand, R.P, *Asian States and the Development of Universal International Law*, Delhi 1972.
Appadorai, A., *The Use of Force in International Relations*, Bombay 1958.
Bajpai, G. S., "India and the balance of power", *Indian Yearbook of International Affairs*, (1952), 1–8.

Bajpai, K., "India: Modified Structuralism", in Alagappa, M. (ed.), *Asian Security Practice: Material and Ideational Influences*, Stanford 1998, 157–197.

Bajpai, K., "Indian Conceptions of Order and Justice: Nehruvian, Gandhian, Hindutva, and Neo-Liberal", in Foot, R., Gaddis, J. and Hurrell, A. (eds.), *Order and Justice in International Relations*, Oxford 2003, 236–261.

Bandyopadhyaya, J., *Climate and World Order: An Inquiry into the Natural Cause of Underdevelopment*, Atlantic Highlands, NJ 1983.

Bull, H., *The Anarchical Society: A Study of order in World Politics*, 1977.

Chimni, B.S., "Alternative Visions of Just World Order: Six Tales from India", *Harvard International Law Journal*, 46 (2005), 389–402.

Chimni, B.S., "A Just World under Law: A View from the South", *American University International Law Review*, 22 (2007), 199–220.

Chimni, B.S./Mallavarapu, S., "Introduction", in Chimni, B.S., and Mallavarapu, S. (eds.), *International Relations: Perspectives for the Global South*, Delhi 2012, xiii–xxiv.

Chimni, B.S, "Retrieving 'Other' Visions of the Future: Sri Aurobindo and the Ideal of Human Unity", in Heehs, P. (ed.), *Situating Sri Aurobindo: A Reader*, Delhi 2013, 130–153.

Gupta, S., *India and Regional Integration in Asia*, Bombay 1964.

Krasner, S., "Structural Causes and Regime Consequences: regimes as intervening variables", *International Organization*, 36:2 (1982), 185–205.

Mallavarapu, S., "States, Nationalisms and Modernities in Conversation: Problematizing International Relations in India", in Bajpai, K. & Mallavarapu, S. (eds.), *Bringing Theory Back Home: International Relations in India*, Hyderabad 2005, 39–70.

Mignolo, W., *Local Histories/Global Designs: Coloniality, Subaltern Knowledges and Border Thinking*, New Jersey 2000.

Nandy, A., "Oppression and Human Liberation: Towards a Third World Utopia", *Alternatives*, 4 (1978), 165–180.

Nandy, A., "Shamans, Savages and the Wilderness: On the Audibility of Dissent and the Future of Civilizations", *Alternatives*, XIV (1989), 263–277.

Nandy, A., *Traditions, Tyranny, and Utopias: Essays in the Politics of Awareness*, Delhi 1993.

Nandy, A., "The Discreet Charms of Indian Terrorism", in Nandy, A., *The Savage Freud: And Other Essays on Possible and Retrievable Selves*, Delhi 2000. Reproduced in Bajpai, K, and Mallavarapu, S. (eds.), *International Relations in India: Theorising the Region and Nation*, Hyderabad 2005, 358–391.

Nandy, A., *The Intimate Enemy: Loss and Recovery of Self under Colonialism*, 2nd ed., Delhi 2009.

Phadnis, U., *Ethnicity and Nation-Building in South-Asia*, New Delhi 1989.

Vigneswaran, D./Quirk, J., "Past Masters and Modern Inventions: Intellectual History and Critical Theory", *International Relations*, 24:2 (2010), 107–131.

Notes on Contributors

Pinar Bilgin is a Professor of International Relations and Head of Department of Political Science and Public Administration at Bilkent University, Ankara.

Gunther Hellmann is Professor of Political Science and Principal Investigator in the Center of Excellence "Normative Orders" both at Goethe University, Frankfurt am Main.

Siddharth Mallavarapu is currently a faculty member at the Centre for International Politics, Organization & Disarmament, School of International Studies, Jawaharlal Nehru University, New Delhi.

Iver Neumann is Montague Burton Professor of International Relations at London School of Economics. He is also a Research Professor at the Norwegian Institute of International Affairs, Oslo.

Chris Reus-Smit is Professor of International Relations at the University of Queensland and a Fellow of the Academy of the Social Sciences in Australia.

Erik Ringmar is a Lecturer of Political Science at Lund University.

Ole Jacob Sending is Research Director at the Norwegian Institute of International Affairs, Oslo.

R. B. J. (Rob) Walker is Professor of Political Science at the University of Victoria, Canada. He is also a Professor at the Instituto de Relações Internacionais, Pontifica Universidade Católica do Rio de Janeiro, Brasil.